Shift your view and redefine your approach – transformation begins with a fresh perspective!

ADJUST

YOUR

LENS

ISBN - Paperback: 978-1-64873-499-1
ISBN eBook: 978-1-64873-500-4

Copyright © 2024 by Mister Rivers

All rights reserved. No part of this book may be used or reproduced in any form whatsoever without written permission except in the case of brief quotations in critical articles or reviews.

Published By Writers Publishing House
writerspublishinghouse.com

Printed in the United States of America.

How Shifting Your View Transforms Your Life and Empower Others

MISTER RIVERS

Changing your perspective, changes the way you experience.

Contents

PREFACE I
   WHO SHOULD READ THIS BOOK? I

FOREWORD IV

INTRODUCTION VI

CHAPTER 1 1
   PERSPECTIVE SHAPES EVERYTHING 1

CHAPTER 2 39
   THE IMPACT OF YOUR POINT OF VIEW 39

CHAPTER 3 59
   TRANSFORMATIONAL TURNAROUNDS 59

CHAPTER 4 116
   SHIFTING YOUR PERSONAL LENS 116

CHAPTER 5 118
   SHIFTING YOUR SPIRITUAL LENS 118

CHAPTER 6 135
   SHIFTING YOUR RELATIONSHIP LENS 135

CHAPTER 7 231
   SHIFTING YOUR PROFESSIONAL LENS 231

CHAPTER 8 252
   PUTTING TOGETHER THE PIECES: WHEN PERSPECTIVES BECOME REALITY 252

BONUS CHAPTER: 256
   ARE YOU READY TO EXPAND YOUR LENS? 256
   AUTHOR'S POV: INTERVIEW QUESTIONS 272

ABOUT THE AUTHOR 299
   Are You Ready to Transform Your Life and Empower Others? 300

Preface

Who Should Read This Book?

Have you ever felt like you're circling the same patterns, stuck in an invisible loop—whether in relationships, work, or even just life itself? It's as if you're standing at the edge of some invisible wall, knowing it's there but not quite able to see what's holding you back. Old beliefs cling like shadows, whispering familiar stories, and no matter how much you want to break free, the familiar weight keeps pulling you down.

You're searching—hungry for more. A deeper understanding of yourself, a clearer view of the world around you. But when challenges rise, a shield of defensiveness hardens around you, almost reflexively.

If that strikes a chord, then *Adjust Your Lens* isn't just another book. It's a space. A quiet, sacred space to unearth and question the reality you've been living in—the one handed to you piece by piece over the years without your consent. We'll begin by tugging at those loose threads of fear, assumptions, and judgments, unraveling the knot of ideas that have been guiding your choices. You're not here for quick fixes; you're seeking something deeper. Real, lasting shifts. Fundamental changes to the systems running in the background of your mind—the systems you didn't even know were there.

Here, in this journey, we trace the origins of the lens you've been looking through all your life. Together, we'll peel back layers—family stories passed down like heirlooms, the silent rules that shaped your childhood, the media messages you've absorbed without question, even the language that subtly directs your attention. Each step brings you closer to understanding how these unseen forces have shaped your emotions, your actions, and even the limits you thought were set in stone.

But change isn't easy. It's not soft or gentle. It requires courage. A willingness to face discomfort and walk through it, knowing the other side holds something richer and more expansive than you ever imagined. Reclaiming authority over the way you see the world isn't just liberating—it's revolutionary. It opens doors to dreams that had long since been buried, paths you didn't even know existed.

So, if you're feeling that pull—whether you're just starting to notice the invisible walls or you're already deep into dismantling them—this book is for you. Inside, you'll find tools, insights, and a community that understands the journey.

The question is, are you ready to step through? Ready to summon the courage to peek behind the curtain and challenge the way you've been told to see the world? The choice is yours. And the power has always been within you, waiting for this moment.

Take a breath. When you're ready, turn the page. Let's begin the transformation.

Foreword

Hello wonderful readers!

I'm so excited to introduce you to the fantastic work of my son, Rivers. This book, **Adjust Your Lens**, is like a warm, friendly hug - gently guiding you on a journey of self-discovery with a genuine desire to make things better.

In these pages, Rivers invites you to take a closer look at how you view the world around you. He talks about beliefs, feelings, and how they shape what feels real to each of us. The really cool part is that he shows us we can change our limited perspectives into more positive, powerful ones.

Rivers strongly believes that how we look at life affects what actually happens to us. He encourages us to face changes with courage, pushing us to expand our thinking and rewrite our own personal stories. It's like going from feeling like life just happens to you, to taking charge and creating your own path.

What really struck me is how he shares pieces of his own life journey. He uses relatable stories and examples that make the mind-body connection easy to understand. By the end, you'll not only better understand how our minds work but also feel renewed belief that you can shape a more awesome life for yourself.

Rivers isn't just an author, he's a friend guiding you on an awesome adventure. I'm so proud to support this book that goes beyond just words on a page - it invites you to discover yourself and feel empowered. May Rivers' words stick with you long after you've finished reading.

Peace to All, Brigette Johnson

Introduction

Through The Portal of Perspective

Life is all about perspective. Imagine it's like a pair of glasses you've worn for so long that you've forgotten they're even there. Everything you see—your problems, relationships, even yourself—depends on the lens you're looking through. But when was the last time you paused to ask where that lens came from? The beliefs we've inherited, the experiences that have shaped us, and the filters we've picked up along the way all silently influence how we see the world. But what if the world you're experiencing isn't the only one that exists? What if a small shift in perspective could open up a world of possibilities?

Think of two old friends from the same neighborhood. They walked the same streets, saw the same faces, shared similar opportunities. Yet, one thrives, seeing potential in every corner, while the other feels trapped, weighed down by obstacles. What's different? Not their environment. Not their potential. It's the stories they tell themselves—the meanings they've attached to their experiences. These stories set them on two vastly different paths.

In *Adjust Your Lens*, we're going to dive deep into these stories. We'll trace the roots of our perspectives to understand what truly shapes our view of the world, our emotions, and the choices we make. This isn't just about becoming aware of your lens; it's about learning how to adjust it. Picture an old machine, humming in the background, running the same way for years. Now imagine taking it apart, piece by piece, cleaning, updating, and reassembling it into something more efficient, more capable. That's what we're going to do with the way you see your life.

This book invites you to step out of old patterns and into new, fertile ground where growth can flourish. As you expand your perspective, you'll begin to see glimmers of light where you once saw only shadows. This isn't about settling for surface-level understanding—it's about summoning the courage to ask the hard questions, getting radically honest with yourself, and uncovering the possibilities that were always waiting for you to notice.

Adjust Your Lens is about planting seeds in fresh soil, creating the foundation for a powerful, transformative journey. With each chapter, you'll learn to cultivate self-compassion, build a foundation of meaningful values, and face fears with renewed clarity. No more getting stuck in illusions or self-imposed limits. This is your invitation to reimagine your world with fresh eyes and open possibilities.

So, are you ready to see where this journey takes you? Take a deep breath, release your assumptions, and let's dive into the life that awaits you on the other side of a new perspective. Your transformation begins here!

Chapter 1

Perspective Shapes Everything

We see the world through the lens of all our experiences; that is a fundamental part of the human condition -**Madeleine M. Kunin**

The Night My Worldview Expanded

It all started as a simple movie night, just my wife and me, sitting on the couch, ready to enjoy a love story. We watched as the couple on screen, Jordan and Ariana, appeared to have it all—until Jordan's infidelity was revealed. The twist in the story hit hard, but what we didn't expect was how much it would unravel between us.

As the credits rolled, my wife turned to me, her face tight with frustration. "I don't get it," she said, shaking her head. "How could he do that to her? After everything she's done for him?"

I shrugged, feeling disconnected from the movie. "I think she should just move on. Jordan's actions show who he really is. Why stay with someone like that?"

That was all it took. What had been a casual conversation turned into a heated argument. My wife couldn't believe I wasn't on her side. She sympathized deeply with Ariana, saying she'd feel betrayed too, especially after Ariana had poured so much into the relationship, even helping Jordan with his big real estate deal. She talked about how, if she were in Ariana's shoes, she'd want to make sure the other woman paid for what she'd done.

But I saw things differently. "Revenge isn't going to fix anything," I said, trying to keep my voice steady. "It's better to walk away and not waste time on someone who's already shown he doesn't care.

The more we talked, the more it became clear—we were coming from two completely different places, unable to bridge the gap. Every time I tried to explain my side, she pushed back harder, saying I wasn't understanding the emotional depth of the betrayal. Soon, she reached out to her friends and family, looking for backup. Before I knew it, I was the lone voice in a crowd of people all agreeing with her.

At first, it felt like I was losing, like my point didn't matter anymore. But then something interesting happened. As my wife's friends began sharing their own stories and views, I found myself listening, really listening, in a way I hadn't before. They all had different experiences, and those shaped how they saw the situation. Some had been cheated on, others had seen their friends go through similar heartbreaks, and each woman had her own take on how Ariana should handle it.

Suddenly, it wasn't just about the movie. It was about how we all see the world differently, how each of us carries our own history into every situation. I started to see that my wife's strong reaction wasn't just about the fictional characters on the screen. It was about her own experiences, the fears, and the values she held when it came to loyalty and trust.

As I sat there, surrounded by all these stories, something clicked for me. I realized that everyone has their own lens, shaped by where they've been, who they've known, and what they've lived through. We were all looking at the same movie, but each of us was watching a completely different story.

This moment was a shift for me. I stopped pushing my viewpoint so hard and began to understand that just because I saw things one way didn't mean it was the only way to see them. When I started listening, like really listening, not just to defend my position but to understand where my wife—and everyone else—was coming from.

From then on, I tried to approach things with an open mind. Instead of sticking stubbornly to my opinions, I started asking more questions. I wanted to know how others saw the world, what their experiences had taught them, and how their perspectives shaped the way they lived their lives.

Over time, I came to see that there's no single "right" way to look at things. Life isn't black and white. Each of us brings our own colors to it, making the picture more complex, more beautiful, and, ultimately, more real.

How Our Perspective Was Born

Have you ever stopped to wonder where our perspectives come from? Why do we see the world the way we do? It's a fascinating question, and the answers are all around us.

Our perspective—the lens through which we view life—is shaped by many things. From the experiences we've had to the lessons we've learned growing up, each piece of our life's puzzle plays a role in how we see things. But what's important to understand is that while these outside factors influence us, they don't control us. They make certain thoughts and choices seem louder or more "right," even if those thoughts might not always be true.

So, let's dive into where our perspectives really come from.

Our Experiences

One of the biggest things that shapes how we see the world is our personal experiences. Every conversation, challenge, success, and failure adds another layer to our perspective.

Take Emma, for example. She grew up in a small town where everyone knew each other, and trust came easily. Because of this, she tends to see the best in people, believing that most people are kind and honest. On the other hand, her friend Jason had a very different experience. He moved a lot as a child, making it hard to form lasting friendships. As a result, Jason's perspective is more cautious—he's slower to trust, always waiting to see if people are really who they seem to be.

Our experiences—both good and bad—shape how we approach life. If we've been treated well, we may walk through the world with open arms. If we've been hurt, we may build walls to protect ourselves. Neither is right or wrong; it's simply how life has taught us to navigate the world.

Our Upbringing and Environment

Another major influence on our perspective is the way we were raised and the environment we grew up in. Family, friends, and the culture around us all play a role in shaping how we think.

Consider Maria. She grew up in a family that valued hard work above all else. Her parents taught her that success comes from dedication and perseverance, and this belief is now at the core of how she lives her life. Maria's perspective is that no matter how tough things get, you can overcome it with hard work.

Now think about Aaron, who grew up in a very different environment. His family emphasized creativity and free expression. For Aaron, life isn't about pushing through tough situations with grit—it's about finding unique, outside-the-box solutions. His perspective on challenges is that there's always a creative way to solve problems, and he's more likely to think outside the traditional path.

Both Maria and Aaron's perspectives were shaped by what they learned at home. While Maria believes in hard work, Aaron believes in creativity. The way they were raised influences how they now see the world.

Education and Knowledge

Education is like a toolbox for our minds. The more we learn, the more tools we have to understand the world. What we study in school, the books we read, and the knowledge we gather all help shape our perspective.

For instance, think about Terry. She studied environmental science in college, so her perspective is deeply rooted in the importance of taking care of the planet. To her, every choice—whether it's what she eats or how she travels—affects the environment, and she's always thinking about sustainability.

Meanwhile, Jacob, who studied business, has a different perspective. His education has taught him to think about growth, efficiency, and strategy. When he looks at the world, he's more focused on how things can improve or expand, whether that's in his career or in the businesses he supports.

Both Terry and Jacob see the world through different lenses because of what they've learned. Education has shaped how they think about everything from daily habits to long-term goals.

Media and Influences

In today's world, media plays a huge role in shaping our perspectives. Whether it's the TV shows we watch, the news we follow, or the social media posts we scroll through, we're constantly being fed new ideas and viewpoints.

Take Zoe, for example. She spends a lot of time on social media and follows accounts that focus on wellness and self-care. Because of this, her perspective is heavily influenced by these ideas she's always thinking about how to live a healthier, more balanced life.

Her brother, Lucas, on the other hand, is really into politics. He watches the news daily and reads articles on current events. His perspective is more focused on how government policies impact people, and he's passionate about staying informed and making a difference.

Both Zoe and Lucas are influenced by what they consume through media. It shapes what they care about and how they see the world. However, it's important to remember that not all media is accurate or unbiased. We need to be careful to seek out diverse sources and remain open to other viewpoints.

Personal Values and Beliefs

At the heart of our perspective are our personal values and beliefs. These are the principles that guide us, the "why" behind our decisions.

Let's look at James. Fairness and equality are core values for him. This shapes how he views the world and the choices he makes. Whether it's in his relationships or his career, James believes in treating everyone with respect and giving equal opportunities to all. His perspective leans heavily toward advocating for justice and standing up for those who might not have a voice.

Then there's Lily, whose core belief is rooted in kindness. She believes that no matter the situation, you should always choose to be kind. This shapes how she interacts with others, often putting herself in someone else's shoes before reacting. To Lily, the world would be a better place if everyone showed a little more compassion.

Both James and Lily are guided by their values, but those values are different. Their perspectives on life, on how to handle tough situations or how to treat others, are shaped by what matters most to them.

Same Mind Used Differently

The heated debate over the movie revealed something bigger than just a disagreement between my wife and me—it showed how differently we saw the same situation. Her strong reaction left me wondering, *Why do we see this so differently? What experiences made her feel this way, and why did I see things from such a different angle?* It got me thinking about the inner workings of perspective.

Perspective is like a pair of glasses we all wear. It's the lens through which we see people, events, and situations. It's made up of our beliefs, attitudes, and assumptions that shape how we interpret the world around us. While some parts of our perspective are inborn—like our personalities—much of it is shaped over time by the things we've lived through. Some of these key influences include:

- **Cultural upbringing:** The family we grow up in, our traditions, social norms, and even our economic background
- **Pivotal life events**: Traumas, achievements, disabilities, or major milestones
- **Relationships:** How others have treated us, especially the people closest to us
- **Education:** The facts, opinions, and theories we've learned in school
- **Interests:** Our passions and the things we choose to focus on

All of these experiences combine to form the way we see the world. They wire our brains to label things as good or bad, right or wrong, important or unimportant. And from there, we make decisions and act based on that perspective.

That argument with my wife opened my eyes to the fact that we each have our own unique set of influences. My wife drew her view from her own life—her upbringing, her friends, and her interests—all shaping how she saw the movie. The more I thought about it, the more I realized that if I wanted to understand her, I needed to stop judging her perspective and start trying to empathize with it.

Living in Separate Realities

In many ways, it's like we all live in our own separate realities. Our thoughts are shaped by the way we've lived, meaning what makes sense to one person may feel completely wrong to someone else. These differences in perspective can cause confusion or hurt feelings when our realities collide.

Let me show you what I mean with a few examples:

1. The Team Decision

Imagine a team working on an important project. One member believes that making quick decisions on their own saves time, so they make a big call without consulting anyone else. But the rest of the team values collaboration. To them, this individual's action feels like they've been left out and ignored. The first person saw their choice as efficient; the others saw it as disrespectful. Same situation, completely different perspectives.

2. Career Paths

Two colleagues, both equally driven, have very different career goals. One wants stability, aiming for long-term positions and financial security. The other thrives on new challenges, always looking for the next big opportunity. When they talk about their future plans, it becomes clear that they're coming from totally different worlds. One sees staying in the same place as smart and secure; the other views it as getting stuck. Their separate realities shape how they think about success.

3. Cultural Differences

In a diverse workplace, an employee makes a joke they think is harmless. But the joke, without them realizing, touches on a sensitive cultural issue for their colleagues. While the person who made the joke sees it as lighthearted banter, the others see it as a lack of awareness and respect. Neither side is trying to be hurtful, but their different backgrounds create an unintended clash.

4. Social Etiquette

A group of friends is meeting for dinner. One friend arrives late, thinking it's no big deal—it's a casual get-together, right? But another friend values punctuality and feels frustrated that their time wasn't respected. For one, it's just being "fashionably *late," but for the other, it's a sign of carelessness. Same event, but they're living in two different realities.*

5. Financial Decisions

In a committed relationship, one partner believes in spending money on experiences, like travel and dining out. To them, these are valuable memories worth the expense. But the other partner prioritizes saving for the future, believing that money should be put away for a rainy day. They both care about their financial future, but their different views on spending create tension. Again, they're living in the same world, but their perspectives are miles apart.

Seeing the Bigger Picture

In each of these scenarios, people are acting based on what makes sense in their own reality, but those actions can confuse or hurt others who see the situation from a different angle. These mismatches in perspective don't just cause tension between people—they can create inner conflict, too, as we wrestle with what seems right or wrong based on our own worldview.

The truth is, each of us builds a reality unique to ourselves. We might live in the same world, but we experience it very differently. This understanding is a game-changer in how we communicate with others. Instead of jumping to the conclusion that someone else doesn't "get" us because they're foolish or stubborn, we can step back and recognize that they're seeing the situation through their own lens.

As I reflected on the argument with my wife, I realized that she wasn't wrong—she was just drawing from her own well of experience, while I was drawing from mine. Understanding that we all live in these separate realities allowed me to approach conversations with more empathy and less judgment. After all, we're not just actors in each other's worlds; we're creators of our own. And the more we understand each other's realities, the better we can connect and grow together.

The Role of Beliefs in Framing Perspectives

Everyone sees the world differently because of who they are. Just like how each of us has a unique fingerprint, we all have a distinct way of thinking and believing. Our beliefs, feelings, and thoughts shape how we see the world—like how a computer works behind the scenes while we only see what's on the screen. Our beliefs act in the background, shaping the way we interpret what's happening around us.

Think of it like this: your thoughts, attitudes, assumptions, and even your worries all influence how you see the world. They come together to create the lens through which you view life.

A Simple Example of How Our Minds Work

There's an interesting experiment by career strategist John Marty that shows just how our brains filter what we see. In the experiment, you close one eye and stare at a plus sign on a screen. Next to the plus sign, there's also a circle. But if you focus on the plus sign long enough, the circle actually disappears! It's not magic—it's how our brains work. When we focus on one thing, we can miss everything else around it.

Just like in that experiment, our strong beliefs can work as blinders. They make us focus on certain things and ignore others. We end up seeing only a small part of what's really there, based on what we already believe or think is important. But when we learn to look beyond those beliefs, we start to notice opportunities or solutions that were right in front of us the whole time.

Beliefs Shape Our Reality

When we hold onto a strong belief, it shapes how we see everything around us. For example, if you believe that people are generally kind, you'll start to notice more kind actions in your day-to-day life. On the flip side, if you believe that people can't be trusted, you'll focus on moments when someone lets you down, reinforcing that belief.

Here's the thing: what you believe shapes what you see. If your beliefs change, you'll start to see things differently, and that can lead you to take new actions or make different choices.

As public speaker T. Harv Eker once said, "Beliefs are based on evidence, and therefore, they are subject to change with new evidence." In other words, beliefs aren't set in stone. They're built on the information and experiences we have, and if we get new information, those beliefs can change.

Beliefs and the Stories We Tell Ourselves

Each belief comes with its own set of reasons and justifications, like a package deal. It's why we nod along to phrases like "everything happens for a reason." But here's the key: the reason is usually personal—it's the one *we* create based on our existing beliefs. Imagine something strange happens to you, and you can't figure out why. The story you tell yourself about it—the explanation you create—will depend on what you believe. Beliefs are powerful tools, so it's important to use them wisely. Remember, **beliefs aren't reality, but it's through our beliefs that we shape our reality.**

Here's a secret: *life doesn't create your beliefs; it confirms them*. If you strongly believe something, your mind will look for evidence to back it up. It's like you're gathering proof to show that your belief is true.

For example, if you believe that hard work always leads to success, you'll notice the times when people work hard and get rewarded. If you believe that luck plays a bigger role, you'll focus on the times when someone got ahead by chance.

Believing is seeing because when you believe a thing, you will always see it that way until the belief changes.

Beliefs Are Everywhere

Beliefs are all around us, waiting for us to pay attention to them. Some beliefs lift us up and inspire us, while others hold us back. The important thing to remember is that when you hold a strong belief, you're more likely to notice things that support it. Until you decide to change that belief, you'll continue to see the world in a way that fits what you already think.

Think about different groups of people around the world—religious communities, activists, fans of a particular sports team, or members of a social club. These groups form because the people in them share the same beliefs. If one person in the group changes their beliefs, they might leave to find others who agree with their new viewpoint. It's just human nature—we seek out others who see the world the way we do.

The Same Information, Different Beliefs

Sometimes, what one person sees as proof for something, another person sees as proof against it. For instance, I once saw two people arguing over the same piece of information—one person used it to prove their point, while the other used it to prove the opposite. It all came down to how they interpreted the information based on what they believed.

What's interesting is that it wasn't the information itself that had the power—it was each person's belief about it. This shows how powerful our beliefs are in shaping how we see the world.

By recognizing the power you give beliefs and staying open to new ideas, you can reshape your perspective. You have the ability to question your beliefs and challenge them when necessary. This creates space for growth and change. When you adjust your beliefs, the world looks different, and new possibilities open up that you might not have seen before.

The way you see the world isn't fixed. It's shaped by what you believe. So, take a moment to examine those beliefs, ask questions, and be open to new perspectives. As you do, you'll see how much your beliefs influence your life, and you'll have the power to shape your reality in new and exciting way.

Defining Your World

The way we define things—like success, happiness, or strength—plays a huge role in how we experience life.

For example, imagine someone who believes that being successful means having a high-powered job, a big house, and lots of money. With that definition in mind, they'll measure both their own life and other people's lives by whether they have those things. If they don't, they might feel like a failure. If someone else doesn't meet those standards, they might judge them as unsuccessful, too.

This narrow definition of success can cause a lot of tension. It creates expectations that are hard to live up to, both for ourselves and others. And when reality doesn't match up with that idea of success, it often leads to frustration, conflict, and feelings of inadequacy.

Beliefs Shape Our Feelings

Our beliefs come before our feelings. Here's what I mean: If a stranger called me a made-up word like "bandrid," I wouldn't feel anything because that word has no meaning to me. But if they called me "stupid," I'd feel hurt. Why? Because from an early age, I learned to believe that word means something painful and insulting.

The labels and definitions we have in our minds shape how we react to the world. If I believe the world is a dangerous place, I'm likely to feel scared most of the time. But if I see the world as a generally kind place, I'll probably feel more at ease and positive. Our beliefs are like the glasses we wear that color everything we experience.

Different Perspectives on the Same Event

The same event can be seen completely differently by different people, depending on their beliefs. Take a rainy day, for example. To one person, rain might seem gloomy and depressing. To someone else, it might feel calming and refreshing. It's the same rain, but the way we've come to think about it—our mental associations—affects how we experience it.

For example, let's say you believe that making mistakes is a bad thing. That belief might make you feel anxious or upset every time you mess up. But if you change that belief—if you start seeing mistakes as opportunities to learn and grow—your experience of making mistakes will change, too. Instead of feeling down, you'll start seeing mistakes as valuable lessons. You'll become more confident and empowered to build the life you want.

Our outer experiences are a reflection of our inner beliefs. So, if we want to change how we experience life, we have to start by changing how we think.

A Personal Story: Redefining Strength

When I was younger, I believed that asking for help meant I was weak. Because of that belief, I tried to handle everything on my own—even when it was hard. But instead of feeling strong, I just ended up exhausted and stressed.

Then, when I started having health problems, I realized I couldn't do everything by myself anymore. I had to ask for help. At first, it was hard, but over time I realized something important: It actually takes strength and courage to ask for help. Asking for help doesn't mean you're weak; it means you trust the people around you and are willing to lean on them when you need it.

That change in my belief had a big impact on my life. It strengthened my relationships because I allowed people to support me, and it made me feel more connected to my family and friends. Instead of feeling like I had to go through life alone, I felt supported and loved. All because I redefined what strength meant to me.

Questioning Our Limiting Beliefs

Many of us hold onto beliefs that limit us. We might believe there isn't enough success to go around, or that life is a competition. We might think that perfection is the only way to be worthy.

But it's important to question those beliefs. Where did they come from? How do they make us feel? And do they really make sense?

For example, does making someone upset always mean we did something wrong? Is taking a break from work really lazy, or is it necessary for self-care?

As the philosopher Socrates once said, "An unexamined life is not worth living." If we don't take time to examine the beliefs we hold, we might end up living a life shaped by limiting ideas that no longer serve us.

By regularly reflecting on what we believe—and questioning those beliefs—we can change our experiences for the better. We have the power to redefine our world, see things in a new light, and create a life that feels more fulfilling and aligned with who we truly are.

Why We Defend Our Perspective When Questioned

When someone disagrees with you, it's natural to feel defensive. That's because your perspective—your beliefs and the way you see the world—is a big part of who you are. So, when someone challenges what you believe, it can feel like they're attacking you personally.

Take, for example, a belief in God. Let's say you believe God is a male figure in the heavens who watches over and judges people's actions. This belief influences how you live your life and how you see the world. Now, imagine someone suggesting a completely different idea—that God is more like a form of consciousness, or maybe they even question if God exists at all. That kind of disagreement might feel unsettling because it puts your core beliefs under the microscope.

But here's the thing: just because someone sees things differently doesn't mean either of you is wrong. Think of perspectives as different ways of looking at the same thing. Each person's perspective is valuable to them because it shapes how they understand and interact with the world. When someone disagrees with you, they aren't attacking you. They're just offering a different way of seeing things. In fact, hearing different perspectives can be an opportunity for growth—it can open your mind and help you understand the world in new ways.

The Mix of Choice, Feeling, and Belief

People often have different ideas about how the world works. Some believe that life is all about the choices we make, while others put more emphasis on feelings or beliefs, thinking one is more important than the other. But here's the truth: it's all of these things. Life is a mix of choices, feelings, and beliefs.

Let's say one person thinks that success comes from making the right choices. Meanwhile, another person believes that how you feel about yourself is what really matters. Both are right in their own way. Their perspectives come from their own experiences. The world isn't just one thing or the other—it's made up of many different viewpoints.

We often make things more complicated than they need to be by thinking it has to be one way or the other. But what if it's actually a combination of all these things? Choice, feeling, and belief all play a part, depending on how you look at it.

The Clash of Perspectives

Because we all see things differently, it's natural for perspectives to clash. Think about the times when discussions seem to turn into arguments:

- Couples disagreeing back and forth.

- Religious debates where people argue about what's "right."
- Coworkers explaining how they think a job should be done.
- Family members arguing about what's best for everyone.
- A friend offering advice to someone who's already made up their mind.

These are all examples of what I call a "clash of perspectives." In moments like these, everyone is trying to share their own point of view, thinking it's the best one. They want others to see things their way. But the reality is, everyone has their own way of looking at the world. I have my perspective, you have yours, and everyone else has theirs.

It's important to realize that when someone is pushing hard to prove their point, it could be because they aren't 100% sure of their own beliefs. It's like they're trying to convince themselves by convincing you. But the truth is, we can only control our own perspective. No one will ever fit perfectly into our ideas, and that's okay. We're all figuring things out in our own way.

Embrace Different Paths

Life isn't just about following a path—*you* are the path. You have the power to shape your journey however you want. There's no single "right" way to live. It's all about exploring, learning, and making sense of things as you go. We're all here to share information, ideas, and experiences, and pass them on to the next generation so they can continue the journey.

There are millions of people in the world, each with their own unique perspective. If we all saw things the same way, we'd miss out on so many different truths and experiences. The world isn't meant to be seen from just one viewpoint. If that were the case, there'd only be one person on Earth.

Moving Beyond 'Either/Or' to 'Both/And' Perspectives

One day at work, I overheard two co-workers having a heated debate about what makes a basketball team successful. One thought it was all about individual skill, while the other argued that teamwork was the key. They were really passionate about their sides, but I saw it differently.

I joined the conversation and said, "Why not see it as both? Skill matters for individual performance, but teamwork is what brings it all together. If you combine both, the team can be even more successful."

My goal was to shift their thinking from "this or that" to a more balanced "both-and" mindset. Instead of arguing over which one is more important, I wanted them to see that both skill and teamwork play important roles.

In life, we often fall into the trap of seeing things as "either/or" choices. For example, we might think we have to choose between:

- **Skill or teamwork**
- **Emotion or logic**
- **Idealism or practicality**

But when we think this way, we limit ourselves. Life is full of complexity, and things aren't always as simple as picking one side or the other. Reality has many shades of gray, and most of the time, both sides have value.

This kind of thinking shows up everywhere—in relationships, at work, and even in society.

- In relationships, couples might argue about whether to spend more time together or focus on making money. But why not both? Time together strengthens the bond, while financial support builds security.
- In the workplace, people sometimes debate whether it's better to compete or collaborate. But a mix of healthy competition and teamwork can lead to innovation and success.
- In society, we often see debates about tradition vs. progress. But why can't we respect traditions while also moving forward and making positive changes?

When we insist on picking one side, we miss out on the benefits that the other side brings. For example, partners who don't acknowledge each other's needs often drift apart. Workplaces that don't respect different viewpoints miss out on great ideas. And nations that refuse to adapt can become divided when flexibility might actually bring unity.

Masters See the Bigger Picture

The difference between someone just starting out and a master in any field is often the ability to appreciate both sides of a situation. Masters understand how to balance opposites, like being competitive but fair, or using logic while showing kindness.

I used to think in "either/or" terms too. But over time, I realized that life is much more complex than that. Now, I aim for balance—finding a way to embrace both sides instead of forcing myself to choose just one. When I focus on "both," I grow and improve. When I stick to "either/or," I often feel stuck.

The Power of Seeing Both Sides

We should all be brave enough to challenge the idea that things must be one way or the other. Instead of looking at surface-level differences, we should dig deeper to see where things can actually work together.

When we adopt a more open-minded approach, we make room for ideas that seem to contradict each other. By doing this, we can find creative solutions that go beyond the usual "either/or" thinking.

The Ethical Lens of Integrity

Integrity means doing the right thing—holding strong moral values inside and showing them through honest and fair actions outside. While we show integrity through what we do and how it affects others, it all starts with having the right mindset and values within ourselves. By building integrity as a personal belief before facing tough situations, we gain the inner strength needed to stick to our principles. This inner commitment to integrity helps us stay focused on what's right, even when we face opposition or pressure. It acts as a moral compass, guiding us to behave ethically, no matter the challenges.

When someone has integrity, they don't just focus on what benefits them personally. Instead, they think about what's fair and right for everyone. They consider how their choices affect others and prioritize positive relationships, aiming to do what's best for the greater good of the community.

Building Blocks of Integrity

1. **Make Honesty Your Foundation:** Commit fully to being truthful. Think of honesty not just as a good quality but as the solid foundation on which your integrity is built.

2. **Be Transparent:** Live in a way that's open and genuine. Make sure your actions align with your values and beliefs. Let transparency and authenticity guide you.

3. **Respect Others Always:** Remember, integrity is something we all work on together. Treat others with respect, honoring their rights and dignity.

4. **Follow the Golden Rule:** Treat people the way you want to be treated. Simple, but essential.

5. **Take Responsibility:** When things go wrong, don't make excuses. Own up to your actions and learn from your successes and mistakes. This is how you grow and develop true integrity.

Integrity in Action

1. **Handle Challenges Ethically:** When faced with tough or confusing situations, let your sense of integrity guide you like a compass. Make decisions based on what's right and wrong, ensuring your choices align with your values.

2. **Build Trust:** Trust is the currency of relationships, and it grows from integrity. Make integrity the foundation of your interactions to build lasting, trustworthy bonds.

3. **Lead with Integrity:** As Dale Carnegie suggests, make integrity the core of your leadership. Great leaders inspire others by demonstrating integrity through their actions. Be that example for the people around you.

In a world where right and wrong can sometimes seem unclear, let integrity be your guide. It's not just about how you see the world, but about committing to ethics, fairness, and respect for others. By following these steps, you won't just practice integrity—you'll live it, making it a part of who you are every day.

The All-Inclusive View

In a world full of different opinions and viewpoints, imagine an open door that leads to acceptance and understanding. This section will guide you through the power of accepting both yourself and others. It's all about finding peace and balance by embracing who you are while also embracing others for who they are.

Acceptance

Think of yourself as a garden. In this garden, **acceptance** is like the warm sunlight that touches every part of it—both the beautiful flowers and the weeds. The flowers represent the good things about yourself, like being kind, resilient, or finding joy in life. The weeds represent the struggles and challenges—like self-doubt, flaws, or moments of shame.

Now imagine you are the gardener. Just like a gardener takes care of the whole garden, you need to care for both the flowers and the weeds inside yourself. The flowers and weeds together make the garden beautifully human. Taking care of your garden means appreciating the good parts and working on the challenging parts. The weeds don't make the garden less beautiful—they just need attention and nurturing.

In life, the weeds (your struggles) have a purpose too. They show you the areas that need more care and growth. By facing challenges without being too hard on yourself, you can make positive changes. Acceptance doesn't mean celebrating your flaws, but it does mean understanding that they are part of the process of becoming your best self.

Like a gardener who tends to the garden through all the seasons, **self-compassion** helps you grow. When you patiently care for both your flowers and weeds, you create a place for growth that's true to who you are, deep down.

Key Idea: Think of your life as a garden where you accept both the blooming flowers and the weeds. The weeds don't define the garden—they are simply a part of it that you can nurture and transform.

The Art of Neutrality

Let me share a story about my friend John, who was stuck in a tough situation. He had a demanding job that stressed him out, and he was also dealing with a long-term illness. Quitting his job might have helped his health, but it would've made it hard for him to support himself. Trying to do both felt impossible—until he found a middle ground.

John decided to be open about his health issues with his team while still showing his commitment to his job. As a result, his workplace made changes to accommodate him, like giving him a more flexible schedule and medical leave when he needed it. Not only did this help John, but it also led to new policies that helped others in the company.

Although John still had tough days, he now felt supported by his coworkers, who became like family. He found balance, and it turned his workplace from a source of stress into a supportive community. He even became a mentor, helping others who were going through similar struggles.

John's story teaches us that life isn't always about picking one side or the other. Sometimes, finding balance between two options opens up new possibilities. Like a tightrope walker who stays balanced to avoid falling, John found stability by not leaning too much in one direction.

Stepping Into Others' Shoes

Trish, another friend of mine, felt really hurt when her close friend Aisha started spending more time with a new group of friends. Trish felt abandoned and jealous because their weekly coffee catch-ups were being replaced with rowdy sports activities. She vented to their mutual friends, which upset Aisha.

Aisha, on the other hand, felt like Trish was being controlling. She thought Trish was making it seem like it wasn't okay for her to have new people in her life. The tension between them was building up and putting their friendship at risk.

Eventually, they sat down and talked honestly. Trish admitted that she was afraid of losing the close bond they had. Aisha opened up about how she actually felt lonely with the new group and valued her quieter, deeper connection with Trish.

By stepping into each other's shoes, they realized that the tension came from not understanding each other's needs. After their conversation, they found a way to balance both old and new friendships, and their bond grew even stronger.

This story shows that understanding someone else's perspective can clear up misunderstandings and bring people closer together.

The Mirror of Acceptance

Acceptance is like opening your arms wide to welcome every part of yourself. It's like having a big box of crayons, with each crayon representing a different part of who you are. Some crayons might be bright and cheerful, representing your happy and positive emotions. Others might be darker, representing your more difficult or confusing feelings.

Acceptance means saying, "It's okay to have all these different colors inside me—they all make me who I am."

If life is a painting, you're using all the crayons to create something special. It's not about choosing only the bright and easy colors. It's about using every single shade—the fun ones and the tough ones—to show your full self. By accepting yourself, you're becoming the artist of your own masterpiece, appreciating every stroke of light and dark that makes your painting unique.

Key Takeaways:

1. **Perspective Shapes Everything:** Perspective is how we see things, and it's influenced by all sorts of stuff like our experiences, how we were raised, what we've learned, and what we think is important. Imagine looking through different shaped glasses - they change what we see. So, our perspective shapes how we understand the world around us.
2. **Living in Separate Realities:** People live in their own little worlds, shaped by what they like and how they see things. But because everyone's world is different, they can misunderstand each other. It's like each person has their own bubble, and sometimes those bubbles don't match up.
3. **Beliefs and Definitions:** Our beliefs and what we think things mean affect how we see stuff every day. It's like wearing glasses that only let in certain things and block out others. So, what we believe shapes how we understand things.
4. **Defending Perspective:** Sometimes, sticking too strongly to our own views when they're questioned can stop us from learning new stuff. But when we disagree with someone, it's a chance to learn more and see things differently. So, disagreements can actually help us understand more.

5. **Examining Perspectives:** Being aware of our own assumptions helps us change how we see things if it's making us feel bad. When we look at things from different angles, it helps us understand other people better. So, thinking about how we see stuff can make us kinder to others.

Chapter 2

The Impact of Your Point Of View

The smallest change in perspective can transform a life. What tiny attitude adjustment might turn your world around? -
Oprah

How Perspective Shapes How We See Ourselves

In Chapter 1, we talked about how personal perspectives act like "lenses" through which we see the world. These lenses can make people interpret the same situation in very different ways. Now, we'll dive deeper into how these perspectives also influence what we believe, feel, and assume about ourselves and others. Our past experiences act like filters, adding extra meaning and judgments to things we see or hear. When we understand how this filter works, we gain the power to adjust our thinking so it's closer to the truth.

Let's look at Damon and Dante, twin brothers who both loved basketball and dreamed of going pro. But their childhood wasn't easy. They suffered abuse from their mom and had an alcoholic father. At school, they were teased for their worn-out clothes and shoes.

Fast forward to their late 20s: Damon is a successful entrepreneur with a happy family life, while Dante struggles with unemployment, addiction, and often relies on others for a place to stay.

At their high school reunion, someone asked why their lives turned out so differently. Surprisingly, both brothers gave the same answer: "Because of our parents." It was a lightbulb moment—both had grown up in the same tough environment, but they had chosen to see and respond to their situation very differently.

Damon's Path to Success

As they grew up, Damon and Dante developed different mindsets, which explains their different outcomes as adults. Damon made the decision that he didn't want to repeat the same dysfunction he experienced as a child. He sought help from a counselor to better understand himself.

Through therapy, Damon realized that he had learned to base his self-worth on achievements and success because of his childhood. But he understood that this mindset wasn't healthy.

To change, Damon started writing in a journal and used positive affirmations to remind himself of his value as a person. He worked on believing that he was worthy just for being himself—not for what he accomplished. By doing this inner work, Damon changed his mindset, which led to personal growth and success.

Dante's Struggle

Dante, on the other hand, stayed stuck in the mindset that he was a victim of his past. He believed that his difficult upbringing was the reason for all of his current problems, and he didn't see a way out.

Dante blamed things like bad luck, genetics, and the system for his struggles. These beliefs kept him feeling powerless, and he started using alcohol and drugs as a way to cope. He also used negative self-talk, telling himself things like, "I can't keep a good job" or "I'm no good at relationships." This only made his situation worse.

This shows how powerful our perspectives are in shaping our lives. Damon's positive mindset helped him grow, while Dante's negative mindset kept him stuck. Your perspective influences your beliefs, feelings, and thoughts. It affects the choices you make and the life you create.

The Positive Pillar Who Couldn't See Herself Clearly

Have you ever noticed how sometimes, even when someone treats you kindly, you feel uncomfortable? This happens because how you see yourself might not match how others see you. You may struggle to believe you deserve that kindness, even though deep down, it's what you want.

Take the story of a woman who, on the outside, seemed like a beacon of positivity. She participated in charity work, encouraged others, and spread kindness wherever she went. To everyone around her, she was the perfect example of compassion and generosity. But despite all these wonderful traits, she couldn't see her own worth. She struggled in her relationships and allowed herself to be taken advantage of because she didn't believe she deserved better.

Inside, she felt empty. Sometimes, she even wished she could be someone else. It's heartbreaking to see such a loving person have so much self-doubt, but it all comes down to how she saw herself. Even though she was kind to everyone else, she couldn't recognize her own value. Until she changed her self-perception, her struggles would continue.

A Personal Story

I can relate to this. There was a time when I isolated myself, too afraid to ask for help or show any vulnerability. Even though I loved writing, I was scared to share my work with others. I kept my writing private for years because I feared criticism and rejection. I thought asking for feedback was a weakness.

But then I realized that strength comes from being vulnerable. So, I started sharing my writing with trusted friends and mentors, opening myself up to feedback. To my surprise, their input didn't just help me improve—it also connected us on a deeper level. We shared our experiences, and it made my writing better and my relationships stronger.

By being open to feedback, I broke out of my shell and discovered the power of collaboration. Embracing vulnerability made me a better writer and helped me connect with others in ways I hadn't before.

How Perspective Colors Our View of Others

Jamal's Struggle in Dallas

Jamal was a lively, outgoing guy from Brooklyn who loved being social. He thrived on friendly debates and using his sense of humor to liven up any room. But when he moved to Dallas for a new job, things felt different. The culture there seemed much more reserved, especially in his new office. People would engage in polite small talk, but the spirited conversations and humor that made him stand out back home didn't seem to resonate with his coworkers in Texas.

At first, Jamal tried to brush it off. But as the days turned into weeks, he started feeling more and more out of place. Weekends that were once filled with laughter and friends now felt lonely. He started to feel homesick, missing the energy and vibe of Brooklyn. His thoughts shifted from, "This is different," to "I don't belong here."

The more Jamal convinced himself he didn't fit in, the more isolated he became. Meetings at work felt dull, and he began to dread going in each day. His mindset started to harden: "Texans just don't get me. They're too close-minded to appreciate someone like me." These thoughts only deepened his sense of separation, and soon he avoided socializing altogether. He steered clear of places that screamed "Texas"—like cowboy bars or football watch parties—and even considered moving back to the East Coast just to escape the discomfort.

When I spoke with Jamal one day, I could sense the frustration and anger building up inside him. "I can't stand Texans! I'm done with this place," he said, clearly upset.

I listened carefully and then asked, "Jamal, where are you really trying to go? What are you actually searching for?"

For a moment, he paused, caught between his frustration and something deeper. "Honestly . . . I just want to feel like I'm home again," he admitted.

I nodded, understanding how hard this transition had been for him. "I get it," I said gently. "But sometimes, running away from a place doesn't fix what's going on inside. You take those feelings with you no matter where you go."

I could tell my words were sinking in. Jamal was quiet, thinking about what I had said. "Maybe the people you feel are pushing you away are just like you," I suggested. "Maybe they're also looking for connection but don't know how to make the first move."

Jamal had spent months feeling rejected, but in that moment, something shifted. He realized that he had been holding himself back too. Maybe his coworkers weren't intentionally excluding him—maybe they were feeling just as unsure and awkward as he was. In trying to protect his pride, Jamal had unknowingly put up walls that made it even harder for him to connect with others.

As Jamal thought more about it, he saw that his resentment toward Texans had clouded his view. He had let his frustration turn into broad negative stereotypes about the people around him, but the reality was more complex. Not everyone was trying to shut him out. Maybe they, too, were waiting for someone to bridge the gap.

"That makes sense," Jamal said, his tone softer now. "I guess I've stopped trying to connect with people here. I got so caught up in feeling like an outsider that I shut down."

I smiled. "And by shutting down, you missed the chance to see that they might feel the same way you do. Maybe all it takes is one small step to start breaking down those walls."

Jamal realized that if he kept waiting for others to make the first move, he might stay stuck in this cycle of loneliness and frustration. But if he took the risk of putting himself out there, of believing that people are kind and open when given the chance, maybe things would change.

With this new perspective, Jamal saw that it wasn't all about Texas or Brooklyn—it was about how he approached people and situations. If he opened up, if he shared his true self without fear or judgment, there was a real chance he could build the connections he had been longing for.

Jamal realized that his assumptions about the local culture had been feeding his isolation. But now, by believing in the goodness of people and being willing to take the first step, he could start to feel at home again—even in a place as different as Dallas.

How Perspective Dictates How You See the World

One sunny summer day, my daughter was feeling bored. To lift her spirits, I suggested we head to the arcade. Her face lit up with excitement, and she quickly got ready.

But on the way there, she suddenly said, "Dad, you stink!" I was caught off guard since I had just showered, but I thanked her for pointing it out and kept driving.

When we finally got to the arcade, she wrinkled her nose and muttered, "It smells terrible in here. I hope they clean whatever it is."

Even after we spent some time playing games, she didn't seem happy. On the way back home, I asked, "Did you have fun?"

She shrugged and said, "Not really. I was distracted the whole time trying to figure out where that awful smell was coming from."

As we drove, she kept complaining about the odor. So, when we got home, I sat her down and said gently, "Sweetheart, if you're smelling something bad everywhere you go, maybe the smell is coming from you. Why don't you check your clothes or shoes?"

She hesitated but then checked her shoes—and to her surprise, she discovered dog poop stuck in the creases! She had stepped in it when she rushed out of the house, carrying that smell with her all day.

At that moment, everything clicked. It wasn't the arcade or the car that smelled bad—it was the mess on her shoes! Her entire day had been spoiled, not by the places we went, but by something she carried with her.

The lesson? Wherever you go, you take yourself with you. If you carry negativity, frustration, or unresolved emotions, they will taint your experience of the world. Everything will seem worse than it actually is. To change how you see the world, you first have to look inward.

This reminds me of something scientists call "negativity bias." Our brains are wired to focus more on negative things—like dangers or threats—because it helped our ancestors survive. But when we're emotionally off-balance, this bias kicks into overdrive, making us see problems where there might not be any.

Just like my daughter with her stinky shoes, when we carry negativity inside us, we start noticing bad things everywhere. We blow small issues out of proportion, worry more than necessary, and even see people as unfriendly when they're not. The world seems harsher because of the negative lens we're looking through.

But the good news is, when we work on our inner selves, the way we see the outside world shifts too. By taking care of our thoughts, emotions, and attitudes, we can start seeing life more clearly and positively.

So, how do we shift our perspective?

It starts with an inner journey. We need to take time to reflect on what's going on inside us. Are there unresolved emotions or baggage weighing us down? Are we holding on to negative patterns that might be clouding our view?

Once we face these inner issues and let them go, we create space for more positive emotions—like joy and gratitude. And when our inner world becomes more peaceful, we start to see the outer world in a brighter, clearer light.

In the end, changing our perspective starts from within. By cleaning up the "mess" inside us, we free ourselves to experience the world with more openness, positivity, and appreciation.

How An Empowering Outlook Transforms Your Life

Ever wonder why some people seem to achieve amazing success while others stay stuck in the same place? It's not because they're smarter or more talented. Often, the difference comes down to how they *see* the world. People who have an empowering mindset don't just focus on the obstacles—they see opportunities where others only see challenges. This outlook can be the driving force behind reaching new heights in life.

You don't need extraordinary intelligence to achieve great things. What matters most is how you look at your circumstances. If you train your mind to spot opportunities and turn setbacks into stepping stones, you can move forward even when things seem tough.

Start Small, Aim Big

Creating an empowering mindset begins with the small things you do each day. Success isn't built in a day, but in the little habits you develop over time. Think of each positive choice you make—whether it's sticking to your exercise routine, spending time on a personal project, or learning something new—as a brick you're laying in the foundation of your future. Each brick may seem small, but together they form something solid and lasting.

When you focus on making each day successful, that builds into successful weeks, months, and eventually years. It's the daily, consistent effort that shapes your long-term success.

Relationships as Tools for Growth

Having an empowering perspective doesn't just apply to personal goals—it also affects how you see relationships. Instead of viewing people as stepping stones or transactions, consider every person in your life as someone who can help you grow. That includes casual acquaintances and even those who challenge you or get under your skin. These people, whether they know it or not, are teaching you patience, resilience, and understanding.

Every relationship, no matter how minor, can be an opportunity for growth. By approaching others with an open heart and mind, you'll find that even the difficult interactions can help you evolve.

Turning Hardships into Strength

Life is full of hardships, and there's no escaping that. But the good news is that *you* get to decide how to interpret those hardships. When life throws you a curveball, you have a choice: You can see it as something meant to break you down, or you can view it as an opportunity to learn and grow. With an empowering mindset, even the toughest challenges become tools for your personal development.

Think of every setback as a hidden opportunity. What can you learn from it? How can it make you stronger? When you view challenges this way, you open the door to growth even in the midst of chaos.

Your Perspective Shapes Your Reality

The way you choose to see the world shapes what's possible for you. If you focus on hope, growth, and possibility, your life will reflect those things. If you focus only on problems and limitations, that's all you'll see.

An empowering outlook helps you climb higher in life because it expands what you believe is possible. The more you train yourself to see opportunities, the more those opportunities will come your way. Success starts from the inside—by shaping your perspective, you're laying the foundation for everything else.

Overcoming the Deception of Discouraging Perspectives

Life is full of challenges that can make us doubt ourselves or feel down. But the real danger comes when we allow discouragement to take over. It tricks us into thinking we can't grow or succeed. Imagine discouragement as a sneaky villain that pretends to care about you but is really chipping away at your confidence from the inside. The key to beating it is understanding how it works.

Discouragement pretends to be a loyal friend. It whispers things like, "You're not being realistic," or "It's not worth trying again," as if it's protecting you from failure. But those are only half-truths. Discouragement isn't trying to help you—it's designed to keep you stuck.

One of the biggest tricks it plays is convincing you that all your problems are caused by things outside your control. "It's not your fault," it says. "There's nothing you can do." While this might feel comforting at first, it actually leaves you feeling powerless. When you always blame outside factors, you get trapped in a mindset that says you're a victim of life, not the creator of your own path.

Limiting Your Options

Discouragement also narrows your view, making you believe that negativity is the only reality. It blocks you from seeing the many creative solutions and possibilities that exist beyond its dark lens. But if you trust in yourself and your abilities, you can break free from discouragement's grip and start to see the bigger picture.

Perhaps the most damaging thing discouragement does is hold back your personal growth. It's like a cloud blocking out the sun, stopping you from seeing the possibilities that could brighten your path. Each time you give in to discouragement, you miss out on opportunities to learn and grow. Over time, this can slowly shrink your potential and make it harder to reach your dreams.

But here's the good news: You have the power to change this. By shifting your mindset, you can nurture motivation and hope, even when things are tough. With self-trust and determination, you can clear away the fog of discouragement and start moving forward again.

Taking Ownership and Rising Above

The key to breaking free from discouragement is to take ownership of your choices. When you take responsibility for your life, you stop feeling like a victim and start feeling like the hero of your own story. This shift in mindset allows life to work *for* you instead of *against* you. When you rise above discouragement, you unlock your true potential and see new opportunities you couldn't see before.

The journey won't always be easy, but it will be worth it. When you choose to focus on an empowering outlook instead of a discouraging one, life's experiences will shape you in positive ways, helping you grow instead of holding you back.

Why Do Certain Perspectives Lead to Failure?

In life, people often fall into three groups:

- **The "Go-Getters"** – those who set goals and accomplish them no matter the time it takes.
- **The "Fence-Sitters"** – those who can't decide and don't take action.
- **The "Complainers"** – those who face setbacks or failures and feel stuck.

What makes the difference between these groups? It all comes down to their *perspective*—the way they see the world and approach challenges.

Let's look at three groups and see why some people end up in the "Fence-Sitter and" Complainers" group instead of the "Go-Getters" group:

1. Starting with a False Premise

One big reason people struggle is because they start off with false beliefs. They convince themselves right from the beginning that their goals are impossible or out of reach. These people often wait for the "perfect" time or conditions to start, telling themselves things like, "I'll start when the timing is just right," or "I can only succeed if everything lines up perfectly."

But this is a *distorted* way of thinking. Waiting for perfect conditions is just an excuse to avoid taking action. You're not giving yourself a real chance if you keep telling yourself that things must be flawless before you begin.

The truth is, there's no perfect time to start. Success begins with a strong, positive mindset. Waiting for everything to be just right is a form of self-sabotage. You have to take the first steps even when things aren't perfect, because progress happens when you move forward, not when you wait for perfection.

2. Listening to Unsuccessful Perspectives

Another reason people find themselves stuck is because they listen to the wrong people. The advice and perspectives you listen to can shape your own thinking. Sometimes, people may give advice that sounds good, but if their own lives don't reflect the wisdom they're sharing, you should question if they're really worth listening to.

Success isn't just about what people *say*—it's about what they *do*. A person may have faced failure, but that doesn't make them a failure unless they believe they'll never recover. The real failure comes from adopting a negative mindset and staying stuck there.

If you take advice from people who have a negative view of life, you risk adopting that same mindset, which will hold you back. Be careful whose advice and opinions you listen to because they can either help you grow or keep you stuck.

3. Staying in Their Comfort Zones

We all have a comfort zone—a safe, familiar place where we feel secure. It's like a cozy sweater we don't want to take off. For instance, picture Neil at his favorite café, nestled in the corner with a book. When a friend invites him to join a group for trivia night, he hesitates. It's not that he's uninterested; the idea of mingling with strangers feels overwhelming. Instead, he smiles and says, "Maybe next time," retreating back into the pages of his novel. It's easier to stay where he feels safe.

You have to push yourself beyond what feels safe or familiar if you want to achieve big things.

How to Make Perspectives Work for You

The cool thing about perspective is that it's like trying on new clothes—you can easily "borrow" or test out different ways of seeing things. If a new perspective fits well and makes sense, you might want to keep it and make it your own. If it doesn't feel right, you can simply put it back and move on.

The process is simple:

1. **Try on a new perspective** – Give someone else's viewpoint a shot and see how it feels.

2. **Notice how it makes you feel** – Does it make you feel inspired or motivated? Does it open you up to new ideas?

We've all had those "aha!" moments when someone shares a perspective that just *clicks* with us, and we think, "*I never thought about it like that before!*" These moments are clues that the perspective resonates with you and could be helpful for your own life.

If you know someone whose life or success inspires you, take some time to understand how they see the world. Try adopting their mindset and see if it helps you grow or approach life in a more fulfilling way.

Those lightbulb moments, when everything seems to make sense in a new way, show that the perspective you've borrowed is a good fit for expanding your own understanding and personal growth.

The Power of Teaming Up

Sharing perspectives with others is a powerful tool. When we brainstorm together, we hold each other accountable, share advice, and encourage growth. This type of collaborative approach is often called a **mastermind session.**

The great thing about a mastermind is that everyone involved wants the whole group to succeed. It's a team effort, where people support each other and push each other to do better.

Choosing to See Things Differently

Every person has the power to choose how they see things. The choice to change your perspective is completely in your hands—you get to decide which viewpoints work best for you.

Often, we get so stuck in our usual way of seeing the world that it becomes hard to see beyond our limited view. It's like standing in a forest and only being able to see the trees right in front of you, unaware of the bigger landscape around you.

But when you open your mind and listen to someone else's perspective, it can lead to incredible personal growth. This shift in perspective might start out small, but even a minor change in how you see things can make a major difference in your life.

We often don't realize just how much our current way of thinking shapes our experience until we step outside of it. By being open to new possibilities and looking at things from a fresh perspective, you can create amazing positive changes in your life.

Key Takeaways

1. **Perspectives Shape Reality:** Personal perspectives act as lenses, influencing how we interpret and respond to situations, affecting beliefs, emotions, and attitudes.

2. **Internal Filters Matter:** Past experiences create inner filters that add meanings and judgments to our perceptions. Understanding and adjusting these filters empower us to align with truth.

3. **Divergent Paths of Damon and Dante:** The story of Damon and Dante illustrates how individuals from similar backgrounds can develop different life paths based on their perspectives.

4. **Power of Self-Perspective:** Individual perspectives significantly impact beliefs, emotions, attitudes, and choices, as demonstrated by the struggle of a compassionate woman with low self-esteem.

Empowering Outlook for Success: Cultivating an empowering perspective is key to exceptional achievement. Daily habits, viewing relationships as growth opportunities, and interpreting hardships positively contribute to this outlook.

6. Small Shift, Big Change: Embrace the power of perspective by borrowing ideas from others, leading to breakthroughs and deepened understanding—team up with a *mastermind* of supportive individuals for mutual success. The choice to see things differently is in your hands, and even a small shift can bring about significant transformations in your life.

Chapter 3

Transformational Turnarounds

"Transformation isn't about adding more work to your life; it is about shifting your perspective so life becomes fun, magical and joyful." -**Sheri Salata**

From Restriction to Expansion

Have you ever thought about why life sometimes feels like we're stuck on a narrow path, guided by beliefs and ideas we never really questioned? These ideas—about who we are, what we're capable of, and what we can't do—act like invisible forces steering our journey, often based on things we've just accepted as true.

But what if we started to question these beliefs we've always taken for granted? What if we challenged the stories that have quietly shaped our lives and told us what we can or can't achieve? Think of regular people who faced barriers in their lives until they had the courage to reconsider the stories they were living by.

Some people, for example, have believed that anxiety was something they couldn't change or that a disability was an insurmountable obstacle. These beliefs made them feel stuck, trapping them in narrow labels that limited their emotional well-being, their ability to succeed, and their connection with others. But when they took an honest look at themselves, they began to see new possibilities where they had once felt blocked. By accepting their own complexity, they unlocked hidden strengths and started to grow.

Now, let's look at some of the stories of people who dared to see beyond what held them back. By examining themselves in uncomfortable ways, they were able to change the stories they had been telling about their own lives. They stopped letting unnecessary pain cover up their dreams. In the next section, we'll explore what life looks like when we stop allowing limiting beliefs to define us. Every time we take a deeper look at who we are, we create new possibilities and challenge assumptions that have been holding us back.

This process requires gentle self-examination, like a quiet revolution that cleanses without causing harm. By shining a light on the hidden thoughts that control us, we wake up from the beliefs we've accepted without question.

Mary Always Felt Like Something Was Wrong

When Mary was a child, she had this deep belief that something was wrong with her. This belief made her feel like no matter what she did, it was never good enough. As a result, she felt extremely nervous around other people. Carrying around this kind of negative belief made it hard for Mary to make friends because she was always focused on her flaws rather than her strengths.

In school, Mary spent more time worrying about how awkward she felt than recognizing her own talents. She believed that other kids noticed her flaws too, not realizing that many of them probably felt insecure in their own ways. Inside, Mary had a voice that constantly criticized her for every little mistake, so she avoided interacting with others. She was terrified that people would see her "true self," which she thought wasn't good enough.

Mary believed she had to be perfect in order to be loved or successful. This led her to feel deeply lonely, as she thought of herself as an unlikable person. The more she believed this negative story about herself, the more it became her reality. Whenever she felt uncomfortable in social situations, it only made her believe her self-critical thoughts even more. As Mary isolated herself, her chances of making friends slipped away, all because of the harsh voice in her own mind.

Discovering a New Perspective

In her final year of school, Mary met a classmate named Gabby who slowly helped her break down the walls she had built around herself. Gabby was warm and kind, always sharing positive stories and trying to connect with Mary in a friendly way. This challenged Mary's belief that people would always exclude her. Their laughter and growing friendship helped Mary shift her focus—she stopped criticizing herself as much and started appreciating others instead.

Seeing how friendly and genuine Gabby was made Mary realize something important: her mind had been playing tricks on her. Her anxious thoughts were not always telling the truth. While her background anxiety didn't disappear right away, she began to understand that those anxious thoughts were often exaggerations or outright lies. Slowly, Mary felt a sense of self-worth beneath the worries that used to overwhelm her. She started to believe that her value as a person didn't depend on being perfect.

As Mary let go of that need for perfection, her confidence grew. She learned to see her anxiety as just stories, not solid facts. This new perspective improved her relationships and allowed her to embrace personal growth. She began to challenge the limiting beliefs that had been holding her back. By letting go of false ideas about herself, Mary's courage began to emerge, like a butterfly breaking free from its cocoon.

The Gift of Looking Within

Overcoming limiting beliefs means asking tough questions about ourselves, but without being harsh or self-critical. Clinging to negative labels stops us from fully living our lives, and the key to moving forward is to gently identify the inner worries that seem real but aren't. When we shine a light inward, we can start to welcome all our feelings, not just the ones striving for some unreachable perfect ideal. By being open and accepting of ourselves, we invite the parts of us that are hurting to come back home.

Growth begins when we question the stories that limit our potential. When we ask ourselves whether perfectionism or feelings of unworthiness are still serving us, we start to see how irrational those beliefs really are. Feeling flawed happens because we believe we are flawed. But when we embrace the fact that we're human—that we make mistakes but also learn from them—we can treat ourselves with more compassion and courage. Those extreme, negative beliefs begin to fade away.

Mary forgave her past and present pains by creating more flexible stories about herself. With these new, more accepting stories, she could finally breathe, make friends, and even dance under the stars she once avoided, thinking they shone indifferently on her. But now, the stars brought her a sense of grace and peace.

Reader Activity: Rewriting Your Story

Many of us carry stories about not being good enough, often without even realizing it. These stories act like filters in our minds, making us view things negatively. But if we take a moment to reflect on these stories, we can change them to focus more on accepting ourselves.

Let's start by thinking about how we label ourselves—who we are, what we can do, what our potential is, and where we fit in the world. Asking ourselves specific questions can help us discover where we need to grow the most.

Think about any labels or stories you might still believe about:

- Who you are.
- What you can do.
- Your potential.
- Where you fit in.

This might feel scary at first, but be brave and honest with yourself. On a piece of paper, complete at least five of the following sentences:

- A negative story I often tell myself is . . .
- If I truly felt I was good enough right now, I would feel . . .
- I delay going after my dreams when I tell myself . . .
- I think others see me as . . .
- I am really hard on myself when I . . .
- If I stopped being so tough on myself for . . . I would feel more joy and peace.
- I avoid people because I'm scared they will find out . . .

Now, take a moment to sit quietly and pay attention to your feelings based on your answers.

1. Do you feel anxious, unworthy, or angry? These feelings show which beliefs are ready to be looked at more closely.

2. Ask yourself gently: where do these beliefs come from?

3. When did you start thinking that certain parts of yourself or your life weren't good enough?

4. Did you choose to believe these things, or did they just stick with you over time without you realizing it?

Think about whether these old beliefs still make sense today, or if it's time to update them. Remember, changing these old ways of thinking doesn't mean betraying yourself. It's about freeing yourself. Keep pushing for growth!

Boxed In by False Limitations

Lamar loved spending hours creating digital art on his tablet. He would get so focused that he lost track of time. But Lamar had a family eye condition, and there was a chance he could go blind. The thought of losing his eyesight caused him a lot of anxiety, especially as a teenager.

As his vision worsened, Lamar felt sad about missing out on things like driving, dating, and being independent. People tried to encourage him, saying things like "just overcome it" or "live normally." But those comments hurt Lamar. It was normal for him to grieve the things he might lose because of his vision, yet hearing those words made him feel even guiltier for being sad.

Soon, Lamar started avoiding people. He believed that blindness meant he would always need help and never be independent again. In his mind, having a disability took away his dignity. Instead of focusing on his natural creative talents, Lamar focused on what he thought he "couldn't" do. Deep down, he wanted to take a digital animation course, but he settled for boring jobs, convinced his poor eyesight limited his options.

Breaking Out of the Box

Things started to change for Lamar when he attended an art therapy workshop at the hospital. There, he met Jill, a confident young woman who had been blind since birth. Unlike others who told Lamar to "overcome" his blindness, Jill encouraged him to accept that he might lose his sight permanently. She bravely shared her own journey and refused to follow the negative stereotypes about disabled people.

Jill didn't look for her self-worth by demanding respect from others. Instead, she questioned society's ideas about what made someone valuable. She showed Lamar that his worth wasn't tied to his ability to see. Jill embraced her own creative passions, found joy in new ways of living, and encouraged Lamar to do the same.

Inspired by Jill, Lamar began to appreciate the hidden positives of being blind. He realized that comparing himself to others or to society's idea of being "whole" was holding him back. Slowly, he stopped focusing on what he couldn't do and embraced his love for digital art again. He found community and support among people with disabilities and learned that interdependence didn't take away his dignity—it gave him strength.

New Wisdom Leads to Unimagined Futures

As Lamar let go of his fears and started to see himself in a more positive light, he applied to advanced digital media programs. Instead of feeling trapped by frustration, he faced uncertainty with courage and began to move forward. Vision boards became his roadmap, helping him fulfill dreams that had once been blocked by the negative stories surrounding his disability.

Through this journey, Lamar worked through the trauma of believing that he was worth less because of his disability. He discovered that embracing his uniqueness benefitted not only himself but also others around him. While having a disability is part of his identity, it didn't mean lacking purpose or soulfulness. By rejecting the myths about "overcoming" disabilities, Lamar found real support in accessibility and pursued his passions with renewed vigor—no longer just going through empty motions. Patience and a deep sense of self-purpose are now guiding the next chapters of Lamar's story.

Reader Reflection

Just as Lamar discovered, many of us carry ideas that shape how we see the world—and these ideas sometimes limit what we think is possible. Society's views, especially regarding things like disabilities, often strongly affect the stories we tell ourselves without us even realizing it.

Let's take a moment to reflect on some stereotypes or assumptions that might influence how we see others or ourselves. Consider groups like different genders, races, ages, people with disabilities, or those with varying levels of income. Write down the groups or situations that are often misunderstood or stereotyped by society. Next to each, jot down the unfair beliefs or assumptions that are commonly associated with them.

For example:

- **Disability** = Always needing help, not capable.
- **Elderly** = Not good with technology, slow thinkers.
- **Caregivers** = Boring, not financially stable.

After you make your list, set it aside for a moment. Close your eyes and visualize each group. Pay attention to how you feel when you think about them. Do you notice any discomfort or anxiety? Even a slight tension might indicate a bias you didn't realize you had.

Now, go back to the list. Think about whether these stereotypes actually make sense or if they're just oversimplified labels. Are there real-life examples that prove these unfair beliefs wrong? Consider how society's ideas might differ from the real experiences of people in these groups.

Finally, journal about how these biases may be affecting what you believe and how you act. Do you underestimate people based on their group? Do you avoid connecting with people who are different from you because of these biases? Reflect on how letting go of these limiting thoughts could open up new possibilities and relationships. The way we view the world changes when we open our minds.

Transforming Limits into Opportunities

Both Mary and Lamar lived with beliefs that held them back, but they found ways to break free and discover new possibilities. For Mary, it was about accepting her imperfections and not constantly fighting against them. Lamar, on the other hand, realized that his disability didn't have to limit him. Instead, it opened doors to hidden gifts and opportunities once he expanded his mindset.

Their stories share a common thread: when we believe that we're fundamentally flawed or limited, it holds us back in all areas of life. Emotions like anxiety become part of our identity instead of just temporary feelings we can learn from. We often simplify complex situations by labeling ourselves, which only reinforces these limiting beliefs.

Breaking free requires questioning the assumptions behind these patterns. Journaling, talking with others, or asking ourselves gentle questions—without getting too attached to our egos—can help us break the cycle. If we believe that being "normal" means having no anxiety, we make the healing process even harder by setting impossible standards for ourselves

It's important to remember that our stories aren't the ultimate truth—they depend on our experiences. When we start seeing challenges as opportunities for growth, we turn suffering into something positive. Lamar shifted his perspective on his disability from being a limitation to being a unique way of navigating the world. In doing so, his hidden talents were able to shine, even though they didn't fit society's typical idea of productivity.

Changing our beliefs means rewriting our stories to include challenges as part of being whole—not as something that makes us unworthy. No higher power decides our worthiness. We're all connected through the same essence.

When we question old beliefs, emotions, and identities that we've pushed away, they come back into our awareness. Feelings like anxiety and anger become teachers instead of threats when we listen to what they're trying to tell us. These emotions only seem scary when we hide our inner light and forget to be kind to ourselves.

Facing the parts of ourselves that we've hidden away takes courage, but when we do it with an open heart, we quiet their painful cries. We don't suffer because we feel—we suffer because we avoid feeling. When we allow ourselves to be whole-hearted, the dreams we thought were lost come back to life.

The invitation is simple: question the beliefs that limit you, and use the energy you free up to find creative solutions. If traditional ideas about life really worked, we wouldn't feel so much pain. The old map no longer fits the journey. It's time to create our own meaning instead of just following what's expected.

Digging Into Your Story of Change

We all have the power to shape our lives by questioning the assumptions that limit us. The beliefs we carry act as powerful levers—when examined with kindness, they can lead us to timeless truths and personal growth.

This self-exploration was the foundation of both Mary and Lamar's journeys toward greater freedom. They broke free from the limitations they had carried silently for years. In the same way, we can untangle the ropes holding back our inner light, keeping us confined by outdated beliefs that undermine our dignity.

Let's dive into our stories by reflecting on these seven key questions:

1. What challenges keep coming up despite your best efforts?

Think about ongoing struggles like health issues, relationship conflicts, career stagnation, or financial difficulties that persist despite your desire for change. These recurring situations might highlight assumptions in need of adjustment.

2. Where do you feel stuck in frustrating cycles?

Reflect on patterns where you feel powerless or unable to make progress—mental loops or arguments that keep repeating. Be honest about where you're mentally going in circles.

3. What emotions arise when you feel stuck or limited?

Take note of difficult feelings like hopelessness, resentment, anger, loneliness, or grief when you encounter obstacles. Name each emotion and honor its wisdom.

4. Are these emotions or obstacles facts, or do they carry your own projected meanings?

Question whether emotionally painful situations are inherently true or if the meanings you've assigned to them are amplifying your distress. Is your anger tied more to your perspective than to actual injustice? Are your definitions of success (like money or status) objectively true, or are they subjective measures imposed by societal standards?

5. How might it feel to embrace parts of life you've resisted?

Imagine welcoming difficult aspects of life—like anxiety, grief, dependency, or loss—with curiosity instead of fear. What feelings emerge when you digest them rather than deny them?

6. Where might you still carry societal biases?

Consider areas where you might be unconsciously holding assumptions shaped by external culture—around gender, race, beauty standards, ability, or political beliefs. Are these views overriding your inner truth?

7. If none of these constraints truly limited you, how would you walk through life differently?

Take a moment to release limiting beliefs and open yourself to new possibilities. Visualize a life aligned with your fullest potential, where your career, creativity, contributions, relationships, and self-care are in harmony. This becomes your revitalized vision of life.

Now, commit to compassionately rewriting just one limiting belief over the next month, no matter how uncomfortable it feels at first. Replace fear with a focus on opportunities, turn anxiety into excitement, and transform constraint into expansion. The first steps may require courage, but new growth will emerge. Your inner light is waiting for your return.

Redefining Our Relationship with Change

After deciding to explore life coaching and write down my thoughts, I dove into research to absorb every bit of wisdom I could find. Before long, I was overflowing with insights I couldn't wait to share with the world.

One day, I enthusiastically told a lady, "Life is meaningless, and that's a beautiful thing!"

Needless to say, her puzzled expression turned into wise counsel: "Hey, if you're unsure of your life's purpose, talk to God. He has a plan for you."

Her advice was profound—here she was, counseling the counselor! But my perspective on life's "meaninglessness" wasn't about dismissing purpose. It was about how we define reality through beliefs and interpretations.

In life, nothing inherently comes with built-in meaning. Our lives take shape through the interpretations we apply to everyday events. You are the master of meaning in your reality, and each event is an invitation to assign your own meaning to it.

Life works not only for you but *from* within you, by design. Your neutral stance empowers you to assign positive or negative meaning to any situation, thus shaping how it impacts you. This process often happens automatically, influenced by your general perspective.

If negativity tends to dominate your outlook, you may feel like a victim, as though things are constantly happening *to* you. "Life is meaningless" becomes a call to recognize that everything is neutral until you give it meaning—*you* decide what it becomes.

By choosing a positive attitude, you can create a more meaningful lifestyle. The ability to view situations as opportunities will transform your experience of them. Once you shift your perspective, life starts changing in unimaginable ways.

The power lies in your declaration—how you perceive and frame a decision shapes your experience. Choose a positive mindset, and you'll find meaning that serves you well. Negative aspects will still exist, but you won't need to engage with them. Declare a situation as positive, and that's how you'll experience it.

Change begins with a shift in perspective, altering the meanings we previously held. Change doesn't have to be a complicated process; even a small internal shift creates a ripple effect, transforming both you and the world around you.

For example, let's say you're considering repainting your car. You have two options: view it as the same car with a fresh coat of paint, or see it as an entirely new vehicle, embracing the transformative potential of change. The way you perceive it will directly influence how you experience the upgrade.

Here's a secret: change doesn't require a drawn-out process. **Once you change anything,** *everything* **changes.**

We often create numerous steps during the change process, which delays results. This is a common tendency.

Sometimes, when we want to change something in our lives, we make it more complicated than necessary. We set up a lot of steps and rules, and wait until all the conditions are met before we believe change has actually happened. This drags out the process of transformation.

But here's the truth: changing your perspective—or how you see things—can be easy.

For example, if you usually say, "Life is hard," you'll continue feeling like life is a struggle. But if you change it to, "Life is challenging, and I enjoy the challenge," suddenly, you'll start seeing things differently right away.

It's the same with change itself. If you think change is always difficult, you're making it harder for yourself. Instead, tell yourself, "Change is a natural part of life, and I'm okay with it." And just like that—boom!—you'll feel more comfortable with change almost immediately.

The key is to keep it simple. Change doesn't have to be this big, intimidating thing. By shifting how you think about it, you can make it easier to handle.

When we think about changing our lives, we often spend too much time thinking and not enough time *doing*. We believe big changes require enormous effort and willpower, like we need to be superheroes to make them happen.

But this way of thinking makes change seem unnecessarily hard. We focus on the difficult parts instead of the potential growth that can come from it.

Instead, we can change our perspective and see change as something exciting and full of possibilities. For example, I started viewing healthy lifestyle changes as fun experiments, not rigid rules.

When I thought about it that way, making changes felt like exploring new parts of myself. Challenges became learning opportunities, and mistakes were okay along the way.

This new mindset helped me relax. I stopped worrying about getting everything "right." Rather than trying to control the process, I began to enjoy the journey.

So, the key is to see change as a positive thing to embrace and learn from. With this mindset, even tough times can become opportunities for growth.

Don't Force Change, Let It Flow

Change is like a soft breeze that touches every part of our lives. It's always present—whether it's the shift in seasons, changes in relationships, or the emergence of new ideas. When faced with change, we have a choice: we can either resist it or go with the flow.

However, if we start seeing change as a normal part of life, it empowers us to handle it with more grace. Instead of feeling like we're being tossed around by change, we can take control and guide ourselves through it with intention.

One way to do this is by changing how we perceive things. Sometimes, we see problems as towering walls that we can't possibly overcome. But what if, instead, we viewed them as opportunities to learn and grow? For instance, instead of panicking over losing a job or going through a breakup, we could focus on how the experience can help us grow and evolve.

By shifting our perspective, change becomes less frightening and more manageable. Rather than being swept along by it, we can steer our course and make the most of whatever comes our way.

Our beliefs play a significant role in how we perceive the world. When things get tough, it's a chance to reflect on those beliefs and determine if they're holding us back. If we feel powerless or victimized, it might stem from beliefs like "I can't handle difficult times" or "Life should always be fair." However, by examining and challenging these rigid beliefs, we can start to change them.

When we replace these limiting beliefs with more positive ones—like being adaptable and hopeful—we gain a greater sense of control. Instead of getting bogged down by negativity, we can ask ourselves questions that promote growth, like "What can I learn from this?" or "How can I become stronger because of it?" This shift turns even tough situations into opportunities for personal development.

As we change our internal dialogue and beliefs, we begin to see external challenges differently. We start focusing on what truly matters, following our passions even during difficult times, and forging deeper connections with others. Believing in our own strength helps us recognize that every ending can also be a new beginning.

By transforming our beliefs and focusing on the positive, we can face challenges with renewed confidence and keep moving forward. When we intentionally change our inner selves, we feel freer, even when everything around us feels chaotic. Our perspective and beliefs become a safe space within our minds, where we can retreat and find calm.

Letting go of the feeling of victimhood reveals that we have the power to shape our own lives. Living a good life isn't about maintaining constant stability or always chasing after change—it's about how well we navigate life's inevitable ups and downs. By knowing what truly matters, staying true to our values, and embracing adaptability, we can transform every moment into an opportunity to create meaning and take purposeful action.

I remember a time after a difficult breakup when I tried to force myself to heal by imposing strict rules on how I should move forward. I equated discipline with being tough on myself, and I tried to ignore my feelings, thinking that showing vulnerability was a sign of weakness.

But suppressing my emotions only made things worse. Trying to follow a rigid plan for healing only left me feeling more miserable. What I needed was time and kindness to truly heal.

I learned that change doesn't work that way. It's okay to experience the full range of emotions, and healing often takes more time than we expect. I realized that instead of trying to control the process, I needed to be more flexible and allow myself to feel whatever came up. Rather than avoiding grief, I learned to embrace it as a necessary part of healing.

When I finally allowed myself to feel my emotions and go with the flow—rather than forcing change—the healing process naturally unfolded. I no longer felt the need to follow strict rules about how I should feel or how quickly I should heal. By accepting my emotions and listening to them, I stopped fighting against myself.

Our beliefs shape our experience of the world, and when we cling to rigid thinking, it only creates unnecessary suffering. But when we challenge those narrow perspectives and stay open to change, we become better equipped to adapt to life's twists and turns.

Rather than forcing change through sheer willpower or strict discipline, we can allow it to happen naturally by shifting our perspective. By believing in ourselves and staying open to new ideas, we create space for personal growth. While we may not be able to control change itself, we can always control how we respond to it—by remaining open-minded and embracing new possibilities.

When challenges arise, it's better to approach them with curiosity rather than resistance. Beneath every tough situation lies the potential for growth. And during peaceful times, we can prepare for the next wave of change by staying strong and flexible.

Each moment offers us the opportunity to plant seeds for a better future—for both ourselves and others. By nurturing positive beliefs and remaining open to different perspectives, we can create happier lives and stronger communities.

So, don't force change. Let it flow.

Key Takeaways

1. **Beliefs Shape Your Journey:** Unexamined beliefs can create a narrow life path, limiting self-image and potential.

2. **Questioning Deep-Seated Stories:** Challenging limiting beliefs opens doors for growth and reveals hidden gifts.

3. **Mary's Transformation:** Social anxiety and loneliness can be transformed through honest self-reflection and embracing imperfections.

4. **Lamar's Journey with Disability:** Viewing disability as a unique way of navigating life turns potential obstacles into opportunities.

5. **Redefining Our Relationship with Change:** A change in perspective can create an instant ripple effect, transforming experiences and creating growth opportunities.

Chapter 4

Shifting Your Personal Lens

Change your perspective of yourself, and you will experience a personal transformation -**Francis Shenstone**

A B.E.T.A.R. Lens to View From

We've talked about how our beliefs shape the way we see the world and influence our lives. But there's more to it than just beliefs. Let me introduce you to the **B.E.T.A.R. Formula**, a roadmap that helps explain how what's going on inside of us affects what happens in our lives. B.E.T.A.R. stands for **Beliefs, Emotions, Thoughts, Actions, and Results**. Understanding this sequence is like uncovering why you feel, think, and act the way you do.

Beliefs:

These are the underlying rules we follow to interpret the world around us. They dictate what we think is true, what we think is possible, and what we prioritize.

For instance, consider this: If you believe you don't deserve love, your emotional experience will differ drastically from someone who believes love is something they inherently deserve. The belief you carry influences the emotions that follow.

Most of us were taught that our thoughts—whether conscious or unconscious—are what produce our feelings. I've taught it this way myself, as it's an easier concept to grasp. But in truth, it's not our thoughts that shape our emotional landscape; it's our beliefs. Beliefs are the silent forces that guide us, the hidden motivators that persist long after fleeting thoughts have come and gone. Thoughts are like passing clouds—ephemeral and constantly shifting. We have thousands of them every day, but they only arise in alignment with the deeper beliefs we hold. In fact, thoughts are none other than choices you're presenting to yourself, based on an underlying belief. This is where the B.E.T.A.R. formula comes in: *Beliefs* generate *Emotions*, which then fuel *Thoughts* that lead to *Actions*, ultimately shaping our *Results*. Recognizing this is powerful because it means you don't need to exhaust yourself by constantly monitoring every thought and feeling. Instead, focus on becoming aware of them, allowing yourself to trace them back to the core belief that's either unsettling you or propelling you forward. Here's the real secret**: we don't do anything without a reason, and that reason is always a belief.**

Emotions:

Our feelings stem from our beliefs and give them life. Whether we feel happy, sad, angry, or inspired, it's often because of what we believe. Different beliefs lead to different emotions.

Thoughts:

Our thoughts are like the control center of our minds. They guide our actions, but they're mainly a reflection of what we already believe and feel. Thoughts don't create our emotions; instead, they arise because of our beliefs and emotions. They're often just mental echoes of what's happening within us, as I mentioned earlier.

Actions:

This is where the inner world meets the outer world. Our thoughts, driven by our beliefs and emotions, lead to real-world actions. Whether we act with confidence, impulsivity, or avoidance, our actions are a direct expression of what's happening inside us.

Results:

Finally, results complete the loop. They reflect how our beliefs and thoughts influence what happens in our lives. If we aren't satisfied with the outcomes we're getting, it's usually a sign that our beliefs need to be reexamined.

By analyzing our actions, thoughts, and emotions, we can see where our beliefs might need adjusting. When the results of our lives don't align with what we want, it's time to look inward and change the beliefs driving our current reality.

Follow this B.E.T.A.R formula forward and backwards:

If you're unhappy with your thoughts or actions, start by paying attention to how you're feeling. Your feelings can often lead you back to a core belief that may be holding you back. When you're in the middle of an uncomfortable feeling, ask yourself, *What belief is causing me to feel this way?* The answer may not come immediately, but it will surface if you give it time.

Nearly every road leads back to a belief. And it's not only negative beliefs—some beliefs are positive and serve you well. Hold on to those. But we often cling to negative beliefs too, because, on some level, we think they're protecting us. For example, someone who believes they're "just a shy person" might keep that belief as a way to avoid stepping outside their comfort zone.

The key is recognizing which beliefs are serving you—and which ones are holding you back.

A Real-Life Example:

I had a conversation with my friend Justin, who was dealing with relationship issues. One day, while we were chatting about food, he suddenly shifted the conversation toward his struggles with anger in his marriage.

Justin: "I'm frustrated with Sheila. I'm even thinking about ending things."

Me: "What's been going on with Sheila?"

Justin: "She's just too perfect. I feel like I'm not good enough for her, like she deserves better."

Me: "Interesting. It sounds like your anger might be more about how you feel about yourself than about Sheila. Have you ever considered that?"

Justin: "Yeah, I guess so. I just feel worthless and undeserving."

Me: "Ah, so it's really not about her. It's about your belief that you're not good enough. This belief is likely fueling your anger. Where do you think that belief came from?"

Through our conversation, Justin realized that his parents had conditioned him to believe that he had to be exceptional to be worthy of love. This deep-rooted belief was causing all sorts of issues in his relationship with Sheila. If he wanted things to change, he would have to start seeing his own worth and stop letting his belief of unworthiness control him.

The Power of Beliefs

When I was seven, I stumbled upon something that fascinated me, even though I couldn't fully understand it at the time. It was the idea that our beliefs shape our reality—what we believe to be true determines how we feel, think, and act. This idea sparked my curiosity, and I began paying more attention to my own beliefs and self-talk. I quickly realized that our beliefs are like the engine of a car, driving our experiences in life.

This curiosity led me down a path of self-study, looking into teachings from the Bible, spiritual leaders, and thought-provoking philosophers. What I learned is that our beliefs have tremendous power when coupled with our focus; they govern what happens in our lives. Life reflects our beliefs back to us, just like a river reflects our image.

Expanding on this, I realized that just like we choose what to see in a reflection in a river, we also choose our beliefs. If we believe we're beautiful, we'll see beauty all around us. But if we believe we're unattractive, we'll see things that reinforce that belief. Our beliefs are a choice, and they shape our feelings, thoughts, and actions.

Everything Is Connected

As I studied further, I realized that our emotions, thoughts, and behaviors are all interconnected with our beliefs. For instance, let's say you lose your job. It's natural to feel upset, angry, or worried. These feelings lead to certain thoughts, and those thoughts guide your actions.

In my own life, when I lost my job, I went through the whole range of emotions—feeling down, angry, even like I wanted to lash out at my boss. I even entertained thoughts about ending my life. But here's the thing—none of those thoughts or feelings were based on objective truth. They were all a product of my beliefs at the time. If I had understood that my beliefs were causing these emotions, things might have played out differently.

It's so important to acknowledge and feel your emotions, as they are a natural part of the human experience. However, I wish someone had told me sooner that my beliefs were at the core of my struggles. I wasn't truly depressed, and I didn't hate myself or my life. I just believed I did at the time.

Moving Forward

Understanding the connection between beliefs and emotions is powerful. Once you realize that your beliefs are behind your emotional experience, you can begin to shift those beliefs and start feeling differently. By adjusting the beliefs that don't serve you, you can radically change your emotions, thoughts, actions, and ultimately, the results you get in life.

The B.E.T.A.R. Formula is a powerful tool for self-reflection and personal growth. It helps you see that when you're stuck or unhappy with the results in your life, the solution often lies in adjusting the beliefs driving the cycle.

When you change your beliefs, you change your emotions, thoughts, actions, and results. It's a ripple effect that leads to real transformation.

Understanding Your Feelings

The emotions we experience often come more from inside us than from the outside world. This helps explain why some people navigate significant life changes without feeling overwhelmed, while others may hold onto bitterness or resentment. The same situation can affect two people in completely different ways. For example, one person may feel devastated, while another remains calm and steady. The key lies in understanding that our emotions are often projections of what's already going on inside us, rather than direct reactions to external events.

The truth is, our emotions frequently come from our beliefs about a situation, not the situation itself.

When I discussed this with friends, some understood the idea that their feelings stemmed from their beliefs, but others still believed that people or events were the cause of how they felt. I used to think my emotions were purely reactions to the outside world until I realized that my feelings actually came from within me. Once I understood that my emotions were a reflection of my beliefs, I stopped getting caught up in stories about why I felt upset or how long the feelings would last. Instead, I focused on shifting the beliefs that were creating those emotions.

This realization was life-changing. It may sound challenging, but here's the empowering truth: external situations don't control our emotions or force us to think a certain way. While we can't always control our thoughts, we can choose not to let them control us.

Here's a simple but profound idea: what if our emotions aren't just reactions to outside events, but actually messages about ourselves? Shifting to this perspective can be incredibly powerful because it means that our internal state doesn't have to depend on what's happening around us.

Typically, when things go wrong, or when people frustrate us, we immediately blame them for our negative emotions. We think it's their actions that make us angry, sad, or anxious. But what if these emotions were signals, pointing to something deeper within us?

For example, let's say you have a friend who constantly cancels plans at the last minute, and this frustrates you. Rather than simply blaming them for being unreliable, consider asking yourself why it bothers you so much. What belief is being triggered by their behavior?

It's possible that their actions are bringing up unresolved feelings within you—perhaps a belief that you're not valued, or that people will always disappoint you. The frustration or anger you're feeling is actually pointing to beliefs you've internalized, which may not be serving you. Your emotions, in this case, are not just reactions to the situation but invitations to explore deeper truths about yourself.

Your feelings can actually reveal important insights. Instead of always blaming others when you feel upset, try to view your emotions as signals that can guide you toward self-understanding. Feeling discomfort may indicate there's something significant to address within yourself.

Now, this doesn't mean that others are absolved of responsibility—if someone is acting harmfully, they should certainly be held accountable. But understanding your own emotional reactions can help you uncover limiting beliefs that are causing you unnecessary pain. Once you start recognizing these patterns, you can work on changing those beliefs and freeing yourself from negative emotional cycles.

So, the next time you find yourself in a difficult situation, take a moment to pause and ask yourself: *What does this feeling reveal about how I view the world or myself?* Your emotions, when explored thoughtfully, can lead to valuable insights if you're open to looking inward.

Thinking Deconstructed

Thinking is a sophisticated process that goes far beyond just processing information. It's an act of deep contemplation where we analyze ideas, experiences, and knowledge from multiple angles, seeking to understand their nuances. Thinking involves breaking down concepts, weighing evidence, and considering diverse perspectives to arrive at informed judgments.

Crucially, thinking is also an **internal dialogue**—a conversation we have with ourselves, where we articulate thoughts, challenge assumptions, and navigate the pathways of reason. Through this internal discourse, we synthesize information, challenge preconceptions, and ultimately arrive at well-considered conclusions. These conclusions guide our understanding and shape our actions. Therefore, thinking is not merely an intellectual exercise; it's a purposeful exploration that aligns our beliefs, decisions, and behaviors with careful reflection, allowing us to navigate life with intention and clarity.

When someone says, "You're not thinking for yourself," or accuses another of "not thinking that through," they are highlighting a perceived lack of this deep, contemplative process. To **think for oneself** means to engage in this internal dialogue, to weigh evidence carefully rather than blindly accept someone else's viewpoint.

Next, we'll explore how **moods** influence our quality of life and decision-making.

Moods Are an Inside Job

Taking responsibility for your moods empowers you to manage them effectively. It's easy to blame others when we're in a bad mood, but the truth is that our moods originate from within us—we create them. When you're in a bad mood, it's often because your thoughts are fixated on external events rather than internal feelings. Your attitude, in turn, reflects those thoughts, which reinforce the underlying beliefs driving the mood.

By owning up to your moods and recognizing that they come from within—not from other people—you're better equipped to handle them. Negative moods usually arise when we focus on outside circumstances instead of paying attention to the emotions within. Your attitude mirrors your thoughts, which are linked to the core belief creating that mood.

When we take responsibility for our moods, we gain control over how we respond to them, rather than allowing them to control us. This shift not only helps us improve our emotional well-being but also strengthens our relationships.

Many couples or families make the mistake of blaming each other for their moods. For example, my wife would sometimes slam kitchen cabinets. Instead of asking her what was wrong, I assumed it was my fault, that I had said or done something to upset her.

One day, I chose to respond differently. Rather than making assumptions, I asked her, "Is something bothering you?" To my surprise, she responded, "I have a lot on my mind, and I don't expect you to understand." She wasn't blaming me at all.

This simple exchange taught me an important lesson: by taking responsibility for our own moods, we not only control our emotions better but also improve our relationships. When we acknowledge that our moods are our own, we gain the power to manage them, leading to healthier and more understanding connections with those around us.

Attitude Adjustment

Just as a well-trained dog follows its owner's lead, our attitudes follow our thoughts and feelings. But while we may not be able to control every thought that crosses our mind, we can control the attitudes we adopt in response. Attitude is the filter through which we see and interpret our experiences, and it has a powerful impact on how we think, feel, and act.

When we choose a positive, resilient attitude, we're more likely to feel uplifted emotions—freedom, satisfaction, happiness, and relief. But when we slip into a negative attitude, it can make us feel sluggish, ineffective, or even worthless. Often, this shift in attitude happens quietly, without us even noticing. But over time, a habit of negative attitudes can become a downward spiral, pulling our thoughts, emotions, and actions along with it.

Think of your mind as a train running on tracks, with your attitude as the conductor. When your attitude is balanced and constructive, the train runs smoothly, carrying you forward toward your goals. However, when your attitude veers toward negativity, it's like the train slipping off the tracks, leaving you stuck or even thrown off course.

Imagine that this train operator (your attitude) is suddenly overwhelmed by emotions like frustration, resentment, or defeat. These strong, unchecked emotions can derail your attitude entirely, throwing your mind into chaos: disordered thoughts, irrational perceptions, and impulsive behavior. If we allow this derailment to continue unchecked, it can affect all aspects of our lives—relationships, work, physical health, and overall well-being.

To prevent this, we must learn to be the conscious conductors of our attitudes, mastering our inner responses and keeping the train on track. This doesn't mean suppressing or ignoring negative feelings; it means cultivating an attitude that helps us work through them constructively rather than letting them control us.

A single thought, if left unchecked, can spark emotions that lead us to act out of character. In the past, for example, when anger took hold of my attitude, it would control my actions. I'd slam doors, punch walls, even break my own phone—behaviors that, looking back, seem almost absurd. It's amazing how much power a single emotion-driven attitude can have over us.

But once I recognized that I could choose my attitude, I gained a new level of control. Instead of letting anger dictate my response, I learned to pause and adjust my attitude before reacting. Acting out of anger without reflection often leads to regrets. By taking a moment to process the feeling, I could choose a calmer, more thoughtful response.

The key takeaway here is that our attitudes are shaped by our thoughts and emotions, and they can either guide us toward constructive action or push us into destructive behavior. By becoming aware of our attitudes, we gain the ability to pause, reflect, and choose responses that align with our true values, rather than being driven by a temporary emotion.

Think of your emotions as signals or cues to help you readjust your attitude. When anger, sadness, or frustration arises, treat it like a flashing "Don't Walk" sign at a crosswalk. It's a signal to pause—it's not the right time to act. Instead of reacting impulsively, let the feeling pass, reflect on what it's telling you, and decide how to move forward once your attitude is back on track.

This means staying quiet when anger flares up, avoiding unnecessary arguments, and, most importantly, not letting a temporary emotion guide your actions. Allow intense feelings to subside, and give yourself the space to choose an attitude that aligns with who you want to be. With practice, adjusting your attitude becomes easier, and your responses become more thoughtful and intentional.

Remember, it's not about suppressing or denying your emotions. Feelings like anger, disappointment, or frustration are natural and often necessary signals. But your attitude—the way you choose to approach these feelings—determines whether they lead to growth or chaos.

Wisdom Over Ego

Personal reflection often reveals how we can better support others. Let me share a story about how negative thoughts, fueled by ego, can damage both a career and a friendship.

Years ago, I worked with a guy named Dawson. We bonded over our shared passion for marketing, and although the job was temporary, we promised to stay friends because of how well we got along. Dawson later landed an incredible sales job, earning about $250,000 a year. But when the company faced financial struggles, he was laid off. This hit him hard—emotionally, and soon after, mentally. Dawson became depressed and lost his confidence.

Over the next few years, he began to withdraw from his friends, making poor choices that only worsened his situation. His ego convinced him that losing his job meant he was worthless. An internal voice of self-judgment grew louder, drowning out any positive thoughts he once had.

When we eventually reconnected, Dawson was a shadow of his former self, lost and struggling to figure out his next step. The bright, creative individual I once knew had become consumed by self-doubt.

As his friend, I knew I had to address his mindset before any real improvement could happen. Our thoughts hold power—they can uplift us or bring us down.

I told Dawson, "Stop measuring your self-worth by external things like your job or your salary. Your inner light and value never left you." He had simply lost sight of his goals by focusing outward rather than inward during those difficult years.

I explained, "Breaking free from the shadow of your ego and unlocking your potential starts with understanding that self-judgment is far more damaging than any setback. Each of us has something unique to offer, but we must clear away doubts to see it. Your abilities are still there; you just need to let go of old, limiting beliefs."

Discovering Your True Self Beyond the Ego

To truly thrive, it's crucial to distinguish between the version of yourself shaped by societal expectations and your true inner self, which is guided by wisdom. This awareness quiets the distracting noise in your mind.

The ego, shaped by childhood upbringing, social pressures, and parental teachings, creates a version of yourself that seeks approval from others. But this ego-self often prevents real connections and growth. As the philosopher Sydney Banks once said, "Ego is only what you think you are and what you think of life, nothing more, nothing less."

Beyond the ego lies your true self, the part of you that draws well-being from a deeper, more mysterious source—the essence of life itself. When you loosen the ego's grip, fresh ideas emerge, allowing your wise inner self to naturally blossom. The ego exists alongside this inner wisdom, but the key is to uncover and connect with what's already within you.

For Dawson, his successful career fed his ego but obscured the inner truths that whispered wisdom, even as his achievements were measured in dollars. His outer success masked his inner light until adversity revealed that his ego was more fragile than he realized.

The solid foundation Dawson had been desperately seeking was within him the entire time. Once he stopped acting out of ego and chasing society's expectations, he rediscovered the confident marketing leader he truly was—beyond the credentials and external validations. His potential had always been there, patiently waiting for him to realize it.

Wisdom's Soft Voice

Wisdom often guides us in quiet, subtle ways when we remain open and attentive—offering gentle nudges to help us get back on track. For Dawson, that nudge came in the form of a video, which felt like it was meant just for him.

Previously, I had suggested to Dawson, "If you quiet the busy thoughts in your mind, your real inner truth will emerge. Ask for clarity from a trusted source." Although he shrugged it off at the time, he decided to give it a try.

The video was titled **"Don't Wait for the Right Opportunity; Become the Right Person."** Dawson paused. Instead of waiting for life to meet his expectations, he realized it was time to evolve into someone adaptable—ready for any situation.

Dawson quickly understood that true happiness could only come from within. His real power lay in consciously becoming a bolder version of himself, guided by wisdom instead of fear.

Certain messages have the power to change our lives—if we take responsibility, no matter what happens. Too often, people focus on controlling external circumstances, like finding the perfect partner, without working on becoming the ideal partner themselves.

Imagine how relationships could improve if we first turned inward.

Ask yourself, *"Would I want to be with someone just like me?"*

If the answer is no, it's time for self-reflection, regardless of what others are doing. The journey is about preparing yourself first, not waiting for anyone else to change.

Life constantly whispers its guidance if we are willing to listen to our inner voice. We're ready to show our best selves once we stop insisting that external conditions must look a certain way. Wisdom is waiting behind the very doors where we once placed blame. Are you ready to turn the key and discover the treasures within you that have been there all along?

Being Responsible

When it comes to personal growth, responsibility is key. This doesn't mean trying to control everything around you, but rather being fully accountable for your own actions and presence. You owe it to yourself and your loved ones to be fully engaged, to show up with intention, and to remain aware of how you contribute to your own life.

While we can't control every situation, we can take charge of how we respond. This kind of personal responsibility keeps us grounded, no matter what life throws our way.

To embrace responsibility, start by keeping the promises you make. Treat your commitments—whether to yourself or to others—with importance. A practical way to stay on track is by writing things down, making to-do lists, and regularly checking your progress.

Next, engage in honest self-reflection. Take the time to look inward and assess your strengths and weaknesses with sincerity. Be upfront about what you discover, especially when stepping outside your comfort zone. If self-reflection is difficult, seek out people who encourage and support your growth.

When life becomes challenging, it's crucial to keep hope alive. Balance working toward your goals with activities that bring you joy. This clarity of purpose helps you stay committed and finish what you've started. There's a deep sense of satisfaction that comes with accomplishing your goals.

It can be hard to stay focused, especially when distractions or setbacks arise. That's why it's important to surround yourself with people who inspire you to grow. However, don't react to every small issue that comes up. Instead, create a vision that aligns with your deeper goals and stay focused on that. As your plan unfolds, let your inner wisdom guide you. Where are you being called to shine?

Give your best effort with courage, even when things get tough. Stay hopeful and don't take life too seriously. Spread joy to others while diligently pursuing your well-thought-out goals. And most importantly, follow through on what you start—communicate clearly, and be reliable.

By taking responsibility in these ways, you become a dependable partner to yourself and others, able to thrive even amid chaos. It's about striving to be your best self and living fully in the present moment. Not just reacting, but creating a vision that aligns with where you want to go. Responsibility means following the path your inner wisdom has been guiding you on all along. Where is your calling to shine brightest?

Mastering Your Life

The secret to handling life well lies in truly knowing ourselves. It's about operating from a place of inner peace and wisdom, rather than letting our reactive ego run the show. While the ego helped us stay alert and survive when we were younger, our true self connects us with what is real and authentic. Being self-aware in each moment allows us to choose the path that aligns with our deeper truth.

Think about how much you can accomplish when you're laser-focused on a specific goal. Whatever captures your full attention becomes your reality. Life works the same way—what you choose to focus on shapes your entire worldview.

Tony Robbins once illustrated this point by asking his audience to count all the blue objects in a room. But later, when he asked them about the brown objects, people struggled because they were so focused on finding blue that they missed everything else.

The lesson is simple: where you point your attention determines how you perceive the world. By intentionally choosing to focus on the positive aspects of situations and nurturing our inner wisdom, we can turn all experiences into opportunities for growth and fulfillment.

This doesn't mean ignoring problems or pretending they don't exist. Some issues require our attention and effort to be resolved. But being self-aware allows us to shift our perspective so we can see the whole picture, rather than feeling trapped as a victim of circumstances.

Life begins to make sense when we open our minds to deeper understanding. Every challenge we face carries a hidden lesson, a bigger truth that's waiting to be revealed if we look beyond the surface. What are your current difficulties trying to teach you about your bigger journey?

Six Signs Your Perspective Is Changing and You're Becoming a Better Person

1. Inner Peace Boost:

You find that your inner calmness and love remain intact, even when life gets chaotic. When issues arise, you're able to center yourself beyond troubling thoughts and choose kindness despite the storms. Your inner light stays strong, unaffected by external turmoil.

2. Taking Charge of Yourself:

Instead of trying to control everything around you, you're now able to control your reactions and actions. You make positive choices that align with your vision, no longer driven by fear or ego. As the poet Rumi said, "Yesterday I was clever, so I wanted to change the world. Today I am wise, so I am changing myself."

3. Embracing Lessons from Challenges:

You see every experience, even the tough ones, as opportunities to grow and learn. Challenges, whether conflicts or setbacks, become teachers rather than roadblocks. You now recognize that every difficulty provides ingredients for your personal evolution.

4. Building a Supportive Community:

You create connections where openness is welcomed, not judged. You validate others' feelings and foster spaces that support healing and empowerment. In your relationships, judgment takes a back seat to compassion, and together you nurture an environment of mutual growth.

5. Adding Fun to Life:

As your perspective shifts, you bring more humor and lightness into everyday life. The energy around you feels less heavy, and problems seem less overwhelming. You find moments to laugh, play, and enjoy the journey, even in the midst of challenge.

6. Being Present in the Moment:

You stay fully engaged in each moment, no longer lost in thoughts about the past or future. Whether in conversation or in daily activities, you give your full attention with intention, making the most of every interaction.

By developing these qualities, you're better equipped to navigate life's ups and downs without feeling overwhelmed. Your progress is measured by your inner growth, not just by external circumstances. What wisdom is waiting to be awakened within you.

Key Takeaways

1. **What You Believe Shapes Your Life:** Understanding the B.E.T.A.R Formula (Beliefs, Emotions, Thoughts, Actions, Results) is like having a secret code to unlock how our beliefs shape how we experience the world. If you change disempowering beliefs, you can actually change how your life unfolds.
2. **Emotions are Like Your Energy:** Our emotions, like feeling happy, sad, or angry, come from what we believe. They're like the energy that brings our beliefs to life. Knowing that emotions are connected to what we believe gives us the power to handle and change how we feel.
3. **Thoughts and Actions Connect to Feelings:** Our thoughts are like a control room that guides what we do based on how we feel. But here's the catch – thoughts mostly show what we already believed and felt. So, our actions in the real world are influenced by our beliefs and emotions.
4. **What Happens Shows What You Believe:** The things that happen in your life, whether good or bad, are like proof of what you believe and think. If you're not happy with what's happening, it's like a signal telling you to check and maybe change what you truly believe inside.

5. **Taking Charge and Changing Inside:** Being responsible for what you believe and how it affects your life is super important. Take Justin, for example. When he realized and dealt with what he deeply believed, it transformed how he felt inside, and that led to positive changes in his outer life.

By using the B.E.T.A.R Lens, you can guide what you believe, how you feel, what you think, how you act, and what happens in your life. It's like a roadmap to help you grow personally and make your life more satisfying.

Chapter 5

Shifting Your Spiritual Lens

We are not human beings having a spiritual experience; we are spiritual beings having a human experience - **Pierre Teilhard de Chardin**

Seeing with the Soul's Wisdom

People understand God in various ways based on their backgrounds. Some see God as a loving being deeply involved in their lives, while others view God as an energy that created the universe. Rather than debating which view is right or wrong, we could accept that human explanations about something so mysterious have limitations. Though people picture or describe God differently, deep down, they often point to the same core idea: that a higher power exists behind life.

Insisting that one explanation of God is the only truth often leads to division. But by sharing our experiences and listening to different perspectives about God with open hearts, we can foster unity. No one can fully explain something as vast as the power that created the world. That same beautiful force touches our lives in unique ways. Respecting this diversity of understanding is more important than proving whose version is closest to the truth.

Religions describe God in dramatically different ways, but many share a common message: the presence of a loving spiritual power behind life. With humility, we can recognize that while paths differ, the destination feels similar for sincere spiritual seekers. There's room for everyone to feel connected with the divine and to share gifts from an infinite source that flows uniquely through each soul.

Although religions may use different words, symbols, and practices to describe God, many convey the same ideas about love and unity. A Christian might feel loved and cared for by God like a protective parent, just as a Hindu might find comfort in a motherly Goddess during difficult times. Beneath these different images, common threads begin to appear. Christians seeking closeness to God through quiet prayer share a similar desire for inner peace with Buddhists who meditate. And in deep spiritual states, followers of various faiths often describe feelings of perfect bliss and oneness, sometimes even using similar language.

This suggests that the loving presence sensed during special moments goes beyond the names and concepts we use to describe it. What truly matters is the experience that touches our hearts, not the theories crafted later to explain it.

For many, the stories and symbols of their religion carry profound meaning and help them feel connected to spiritual guidance. The key is to embrace the love shared by various faiths while also respecting each culture's unique way of expressing it. By staying open to different beliefs, we can discover shared truths. Our soul's longing for connection with the boundless spirit can be satisfied, no matter what name we use to describe it.

During special spiritual moments, people from different religions describe the same sense of perfect peace, joy, or inner quiet. The feeling of being a separate self fade away. A Muslim chanting Allah's holy name may experience a sense of unity, just as a Hindu meditating on the true self may recognize the temporary nature of the ego. Christians and Quakers often speak of moments of connection with a brilliant inner light.

Seeing another person's spiritual path as equally precious yet unique allows us to avoid the judgment of whose faith is higher or lower. One wise teacher's insights may complement another's blind spots. By humbly sharing different viewpoints, everyone's understanding can grow. While our beliefs may use different symbols, many paths ascend the same mountain.

My doubts about faith began to fade after a close friendship with a devoted Muslim. Watching his heart shine as he spoke about the Prophet showed me the authentic power of religion when it aligns with someone's personality and inner truth. His example revealed that real spiritual wisdom lives beyond rigid rules. Through friendships with spiritual people from different backgrounds but shared visions, my once-closed perspective began to gently open.

I've boiled my religion down to five simple words: *God is, and God does*. These words hold everything I need. *God is*—an ever-present reality, beyond words and definitions. It means that God simply exists, as constant and unchanging as the air we breathe. And *God does*—meaning God is active, involved, moving through us and around us. It's a reminder that faith isn't just about believing in a distant force; it's about recognizing the ways God's presence works in our lives, in every kindness, every challenge, every moment of grace.

In those five words, there's both stillness and action, being and doing. For me, they're enough."

When Meaning Comes Alive

What is the purpose of our lives? Is it to serve God, use our talents, or help society? Maybe it's something spiritual beyond what we can fully understand, or it could be personal, based on what matters most to each of us.

We might find purpose on different levels—perhaps our souls are here to learn through challenges, share our gifts with others, or discover unconditional love. Instead of thinking purpose has to be tied to one specific achievement, maybe it reveals itself gradually, as we become more aware and serve others in each moment.

When we let go of narrow ideas about what purpose *should* be, we open ourselves to broader possibilities. These possibilities align with our unique interests and joys.

Life's journey might be about balancing clear goals with a sense of openness to whatever joys and opportunities come our way. By questioning old beliefs about what meaning looks like and having faith in positive outcomes, we can move toward horizons that lie beyond what logic can explain.

Some people even recall planning life lessons before birth, with the help of spiritual guides. These memories bring a sense of peace when facing hardships because they see a larger purpose at work. As the author Eckhart Tolle says, "Being fully present often allows natural meaning to become clear rather than demanding life meet expectations." When we relax and live in the moment, meaning often reveals itself through coincidences and subtle signs.

Society often teaches us limiting ideas about purpose—like getting status, wealth, or praise. But when we question these ideas, we can embrace callings like bringing joy through music, supporting loved ones, or volunteering. Purpose becomes wider and richer when we let go of the "shoulds" imposed by others.

Feeling empty or depressed often happens when we measure our worth by possessions or social status instead of by things like good relationships, personal growth, and helping our community. True meaning comes from expressing our unique gifts and showing compassion.

In Japanese philosophy, there's a concept called **Ikigai**—finding the place where your talents, passions, and sense of mission intersect. This naturally uncovers a deep sense of purpose. It happens when we combine doing what we love with serving others.

Meaning in life unfolds differently for each of us, but there are patterns that guide us. What brings us joy? When do we lose track of time because we're so immersed in something? Often, the activities that make time fly by are clues to our purpose.

Ironically, purpose often becomes clearest when we stop chasing it. Setting aside quiet time to reflect allows insights to surface naturally. Like when we were children, life's meaning evolves across different stages—first through play and learning, then through productivity, and later through leaving a legacy or mentoring others. Seeing life as a whole lets purpose unfold naturally, without needing to force it.

While purpose starts within us, it becomes most powerful when shared with others. The sweet spot is using our unique talents to help meet the needs of those around us. When our inspiration aligns with caring for our wider community, life feels richer, more meaningful, and timeless.

Instead of overanalyzing purpose, we are meant to plant seeds of action and let meaning grow. By following our intuition, fully engaging in what lights us up, and using that passion to serve others, we walk the path of fulfillment.

When we allow purpose to come alive, it lifts us up like wings, helping us soar toward a destiny that is uniquely ours but shared with others. Our greatest balance comes when inner growth leads to helping the world thrive. In this way, we all walk together on an uplifting path that connects us across time.

The Spiritual Purpose Behind Worldly Pain

Suffering is often seen as a mystery from a human perspective. While some may view life as flawed because of suffering, a higher, more spiritual view might see pain as an illusion—a temporary sense of separation designed to guide us back to unity through compassion.

Rather than seeing suffering as a sign of being abandoned by higher powers, it can be seen as carrying hidden wisdom. On an individual level, suffering can help break down our egos and unhealthy patterns. On a collective level, it forces us to expand our moral awareness, helping us include and care for those who have been marginalized. Growth often comes through struggle and hardship.

Though we must acknowledge the immense suffering in the world, an elevated perspective reveals that powerful forces can create light even from darkness. The Buddha taught that pain and pleasure are two sides of the same coin. While human suffering seems unfair or cruel, a higher consciousness may allow and eventually transform all experiences, even painful ones.

Many mystics speak of a loving awareness at the heart of creation. This awareness optimizes conditions for our growth, which sometimes requires us to experience deep suffering in order to grow in compassion and wisdom. It's like a crucible that burns away illusions and opens us to deeper truths.

Instead of asking, "How could a loving God allow this?" perhaps transcending suffering requires surrendering our need for answers and trusting that there's a larger plan at work. Peace and renewed faith may come from accepting that not everything makes sense from our limited human view.

Some spiritual beliefs suggest that we chose to be born into this turbulent time to learn and grow through shared global challenges. Before birth, our souls may have agreed to face hardships to spur greater compassion and growth.

For instance, my friend Ciara kept attracting unhealthy relationships until a devastating loss finally forced her to let go of her ego. That painful experience helped her see beyond her assumptions and touch her deeper purpose. She realized her calling was to forgive herself and guide others who had suffered similar traumas.

As the poet Rumi said, "The wound is where the light enters you." Pain may be part of a divine plan to help us grow and evolve. Suffering lifts us, helping us connect the moments of our lives into a greater sense of unity and understanding.

The Guru Within You

Some believe that truth can only be found by strictly following certain teachers, texts, or rituals. However, life offers wisdom in many ways, and no one person or path holds the absolute truth. Each of us walks a unique spiritual journey.

Instead of constantly looking for answers outside of yourself, try looking inward. Beyond your thoughts and emotions, what is the true essence of who you are? By regularly reflecting on this, you'll discover that truth is already within you—not found in external things or fleeting experiences.

Instead of getting caught up in emotions or dramas, learn to observe events from a place of stillness within yourself. Identities and situations come and go, but you—the formless observer—remain unchanged.

The realization you seek is already within you. By gently looking inward, you'll connect with the source of true knowledge. Stay open, keep exploring, and trust that inner truth will emerge naturally over time.

Many spiritual seekers get caught up in chasing mystical experiences or visions of universal oneness. However, becoming too attached to these experiences can distract you from the deeper truth. It's like focusing on the finger pointing at the moon instead of looking at the moon itself.

Some teachers may encourage dependency on external rituals or texts, but the best guides help you nurture your own inner wisdom. Be mindful of who you follow and whether they encourage independence or reliance.

Ultimately, the sacred exists beyond words, in silent presence. The call is to step out of limitations and embrace the vastness within. You don't need to cling to fleeting experiences when endless presence is available to you right now. Let go of old expectations and discover what is truly here, within yourself.

As you embrace this deeper knowing, you'll cultivate compassion, wisdom, and courage. The journey is one of refining your understanding over time, learning to embrace both the light and the shadows along the way. Every teacher you'll ever need is already within you. Trust that inner flame, which has guided you across lifetimes, and rest in the presence that is always with you. Transformation will unfold naturally, at its own pace.

You're Not Broken; You Just Believe You Are

"You're not broken; you just believe you are." Those were the words that hit me hard during a conversation with a life coach specializing in limiting beliefs. When I first heard the term "limiting belief life coach," I was skeptical. It sounded abstract, maybe even unnecessary. But as I opened up about my background—growing up in a Christian household, my parents' divorce, and my ongoing commitment to self-improvement—the conversation took an unexpected turn.

The life coach, in her calm yet direct manner, cut right through my carefully constructed justifications. After listening to my story of years spent trying to better myself, she asked a simple but powerful question: "What led you to believe that fixing yourself should be your sole focus?"

I wasn't prepared for that. I had always thought of self-improvement as the answer to all my problems. Like many, I had consumed countless books, attended workshops, and followed self-help advice to "fix" what I thought was wrong with me. But the coach pushed me to question whether this constant focus on self-repair was based on the assumption that I was broken to begin with.

She acknowledged that personal growth is important but cautioned against turning it into an endless quest. The idea that I was "broken" had become my identity, she suggested, and as long as I held onto that belief, no amount of self-help would ever feel like enough. "What if," she asked, "you allowed yourself to show up in the world as already whole, as unbroken and unshakeable?"

It was a radical shift in thinking. Instead of focusing inward, always trying to fix myself, she encouraged me to direct my energy outward—toward helping others, toward embracing life as it is. While external factors could challenge my physical well-being or emotional stability, she reminded me that my spirit was intact, resilient, and powerful.

A New Perspective: Shifting from Brokenness to Wholeness

The life coach's words planted a seed of doubt about my long-held belief that I was somehow inherently flawed. I began to realize that much of my self-improvement journey had been driven by a desire to control my life, to perfect myself because I didn't trust that I was enough as I was. But what if I didn't need fixing? What if I had always been whole, just temporarily caught up in human struggles?

This shift in thinking was liberating. I realized that the endless quest for self-perfection had been fueled by a lack of self-trust and a sense of powerlessness. By believing I was broken, I was keeping myself in a cycle of self-judgment and self-repair. And that belief was preventing me from fully living my life.

The truth is, life molds and shapes us whether we're conscious of it or not. We don't need to constantly micromanage our growth. As a spirit living a human existence, we naturally impact the world around us, and life, in turn, shapes us through experiences—both good and bad.

Moving from Self-Focus to Empowering Others

As I began to let go of the belief that I was broken, my focus naturally shifted from inward to outward. I found that when I stopped obsessing over "fixing" myself, I had more energy to help others. It wasn't that I abandoned self-care or personal growth, but I stopped letting those things define my worth. I realized that personal growth doesn't have to mean endless self-criticism. Instead, it can be about showing up fully, as you are, and offering your strengths to the world.

When we stop seeking validation through constant self-improvement, we allow ourselves to reclaim our authority. We can then direct our energy toward uplifting others and making a positive impact in our communities.

The life coach had asked me, "If you didn't believe you were broken, could you show up as a healed person, confident and grounded in your unshakable spirit?" That question stayed with me. The moment I stopped seeing myself as fragmented, I felt a deeper sense of connection to others and to the world around me.

I wasn't stuck in an internal battle anymore, trying to fix what wasn't really broken. Instead, I was free to fully participate in life.

Practical Steps Toward Wholeness

If you've ever felt trapped by the belief that you're broken, know that this belief is not your reality—it's just a story you've told yourself. To start shifting your perspective, here are a few steps that helped me:

1. **Challenge Core Beliefs:** Take time to question the beliefs that have shaped your self-image. Are they based on truth, or are they just stories you've picked up along the way?

2. **Affirm Your Wholeness:** Practice affirming that you are enough, as you are, without needing to be "fixed." Say it out loud: "I am whole, just as I am."

3. **Focus on Others:** Redirect some of your energy toward helping others. When you're not constantly focused on your own flaws, you'll see that you have so much to offer the world.

4. **Develop Self-Trust:** Start trusting that you have everything you need to navigate life. You don't need to control or perfect every aspect of yourself. Trust that your spirit is strong and capable.

5. **Embrace Self-Compassion:** Be kind to yourself in moments of struggle. You don't have to be perfect to be worthy of love and belonging. Self-compassion allows you to see the value in both your strengths and your imperfections.

Key Takeaways

1. **Unity in Diversity of Spiritual Perspectives:** Emphasizes the diversity in how people perceive and understand God or a higher power. It encourages acceptance of different perspectives, promoting unity rather than division.
2. **Common Threads Across Religions:** Despite differences in religious beliefs, this section points out common threads, such as the pursuit of closeness to a spiritual power, inner peace through meditation, and shared experiences of profound connection, suggesting a universal spiritual essence.
3. **Exploring Life's Purpose Beyond Conventions:** The idea of life's purpose is explored beyond conventional notions, suggesting that purpose may unfold gradually through awareness, service, and deepening understanding. It challenges rigid definitions and encourages openness to diverse paths.
4. **Transformation Through Suffering:** This section presents suffering as a temporary illusion, holding hidden wisdom for both individual and collective growth. It invites a perspective that sees suffering as a catalyst for personal transformation

and moral evolution rather than an indication of a flawed existence.

5. **Inner Wisdom and Self-Discovery:** The importance of inner reflection and self-discovery is highlighted. It encourages individuals to look within for wisdom, emphasizing that the truth is already present. It discourages dependence on external rituals and urges a direct connection with one's inner self.

Chapter 6

Shifting Your Relationship Lens

We all learned love differently. So, in turn, we all give it differently -**Anthony Gucciardi**

Nurturing Our Most Vital Connections

Relationships form the core of our lives. Whether it's our family, friends, romantic partners, or colleagues, these connections bring meaning, joy, challenges, and growth. But, just as our bodies and minds evolve over time, so too must our perspectives on relationships. Holding on to outdated views can prevent healthy bonds from flourishing.

In this chapter, we'll explore common limiting perspectives that distort how we see the people in our lives. You might unknowingly be holding on to childhood interpretations of family members, unrealistic romantic ideals from movies, or venting workplace frustrations at your partner.

We'll examine five perspectives on relationships, identifying their flaws and reframing them with expanded views. Along the way, you'll reflect on your tendencies and receive practical advice to improve your connections with your spouse, parents, friends, and colleagues. By the end of this chapter, you will gain insights into:

- Viewing your parents as fellow adults, not just caregivers.
- Letting go of unrealistic romantic expectations.
- Revitalizing stagnant friendships.
- Judging colleagues' intentions less negatively.

Letting go of long-held perspectives can feel uncomfortable, but discomfort is often the first step toward growth. With compassion for yourself and those around you, you can transform how you see your loved ones and, in turn, transform your most cherished relationships. Starting from a place of empathy, you can create deeper connections and nurture bonds that thrive on mutual understanding.

Seeing Parents as Fellow Adults

For many of us, the parent-child dynamic continues into adulthood, shaped by deep-rooted views from both sides. As children, we naturally saw our parents as authoritative figures. But continuing to view them in a role of superiority or inferiority prevents us from seeing them as individuals with their own lives, dreams, and vulnerabilities.

Start by reflecting on the traits you still associate only with your parents' roles as caregivers. Do you see your mother mainly as a nurturer or homemaker, even though she may have new interests? Do you view your father solely as a provider, missing his personal struggles or softer qualities? Recognizing these limitations is the first step in deepening your connection.

Now, consciously try to see your parents as people beyond their parental roles. Ask yourself, "Who are they really?" What dreams, quirks, struggles, or passions might you have overlooked? Take the time to learn about their work, friendships, and inner lives with a fresh perspective. You may be surprised at what you discover.

Finally, watch for moments when you slip back into outdated parent-child roles. When tensions arise, ask yourself, "Am I seeing them through the lens of an adult or a child?" Then, try adjusting your perspective before responding. With consistent effort, you can relate to your parents as fellow adults, unlocking new levels of understanding and compassion in the relationship.

Glimpsing New Parts of a Parent's Identity

Seeing your parents as real people, rather than just "Mom" or "Dad," opens the door to uncovering new aspects of their identities. You may find surprising gaps between who you thought they were and who they truly are.

- **Ask deeper questions.** Inquire about topics you haven't explored before, like their view of life so far, their proudest moments, their biggest regrets, or their future dreams. Ask them what friendships nourish them or how they overcame specific challenges. Move beyond surface-level conversations to discover more meaningful revelations.
- **Observe them outside the family context.** Watching how your parents interact with friends or colleagues can give you a glimpse of who they are outside of the parent-child dynamic. How do they handle themselves professionally? What makes them laugh with close friends? These moments can reveal facets of their personality you haven't seen before.
- **Learn about their lives.** Dig deeper into aspects of your parents' lives you might not know much about. Research their career path, their educational background, or even hobbies and passions they may

have pursued before you were born. This exploration may uncover sides of them you never thought existed.

Seeing your parents in a more human light can be eye-opening. You might discover qualities you admire or challenges they've faced that make them more relatable. Yes, some revelations might be less than inspiring, but understanding the full picture of who they are allows you to create a relationship based on reality, not just old expectations.

As you expand your view of your parents, it can lead to a more authentic, fulfilling relationship—one that reflects who they are now, not who they were when you were a child.

Letting Go of Unrealistic Romantic Expectations

In the realm of romantic relationships, we often carry expectations formed by childhood fairytales or romanticized movies. These unrealistic ideals can lead to disappointment when our partners don't match up to the flawless images we have in our minds.

Healthy relationships aren't about finding someone who fits perfectly into an idealized mold. Rather, they're about learning to love someone in their entirety, including their imperfections. Relationships take work, communication, and a willingness to grow together, not just individually.

Let's explore some common stories and themes that shape unrealistic romantic views so you can consciously challenge that conditioning.

- **The "Love At First Sight" Trap** – This myth convinces us that initial sparks signal destiny rather than simply physical attraction. But deep attachment grows gradually through weathering life's ups and downs together.
- **The "Happily Ever After" Fantasy** – Fairy tales implant the notion that "endings" are eternally happy. Real couples must actively maintain bonds despite life's inevitable changes.
- **The "Mind-Reading Soulmate" Ideal** – Some lovers expect partners to intuitively grasp their every need and feeling without communication. But this psychic connection is rare. Expecting it breeds resentment.
- **The "Perfect Person" Conviction** – Many unconsciously seek clones of parents or idealized versions of themselves in partners. But holding partners to standards of perfection inevitably disappoints.
- **The "One True Love" Belief** – Too often, lovers leave or neglect good relationships while endlessly seeking an imaginary "one" based on superficial traits versus shared values and teamwork.

If you've been holding onto these romantic ideals, reflect on where these expectations come from. Are they shaped by movies, books, or past relationships? How do these ideals compare to the reality of your partner? Start appreciating the ways in which your partner shows love, even if it doesn't fit neatly into a romantic movie plot.

Try focusing on the shared experiences, trust, and mutual support that form the foundation of a real relationship. By letting go of perfection and embracing your partner's true self, you'll find deeper intimacy and connection.

Once you're aware of romantic myths clouding your vision, actively reframe your perspectives for improved intimacy:

- **Redirect Expectations Internally**: Rather than pressure partners to match fantasy ideals, focus expectations on your own growth. Set goals like cultivating more patience, planning appreciation gestures, or deepening your empathy through questions, not assumptions.
- **Celebrate Imperfect Progress:** Let go of measuring your relationship against fiction or others' public personas. Instead, privately celebrate milestones significant to you both – whether that's making quality time, overcoming conflict, or trying something new together.

- **Rewrite Limiting Labels:** If you mentally label your partner in a constraining way – like "distant," "controlling," or "non-romantic" – consciously rephrase it. Perhaps "independent" or "particular in communicating affection" is closer to truth while leaving room for growth.

There are many techniques for adjusting lenses distorted by myth and misperception within romantic bonds. As you shift perspective with compassion and creativity, you pave the way for increased fulfillment and connection.

Enriching Stale Friendships

Friendships can become stagnant over time if we start taking them for granted or fall into predictable routines. You may find yourself having the same conversations or only connecting out of habit rather than genuine interest. To refresh these friendships, shift your perspective from viewing them as static to seeing them as evolving.

Start by acknowledging that both you and your friends are continually changing. Ask them about their current passions, challenges, or dreams. Bring new energy into your interactions by suggesting new activities or shared experiences that you've never tried together.

By being more intentional about deepening your friendship, you can reinvigorate the bond and discover new layers of connection.

Friendships can be rekindled and deepened at any stage of life when both people make an effort. Start by honestly evaluating the current state of your friendships using these prompts:

- What initially brought you and this friend together?
- Do you still see that spark?
- Which qualities of the friendship still exist versus which ones are just memories?
- What weaknesses or stagnant patterns in the friendship bother you most right now?
- How might your friend's current life circumstances be limiting their ability to invest in the friendship lately?
- What's one small step you could take to revive the spirit between you?

Next, set aside embarrassment or pride. Have open conversations with your friends about what's not working, issues left unaddressed, and dreams you can reignite together. With care and courage, lifeless friendships can be transformed into rich sources of rejuvenation for many years to come.

Judging Friends More Compassionately

As we get older, it's easy to judge friends who take different paths in life or don't meet the changing expectations we have for our relationships. We may find ourselves making comparisons, feeling disappointed by perceived slights, or thinking that we've outgrown people we've known for years.

However, friendships that stand the test of time are built on flexibility and understanding. They adapt to accommodate each person's growth, shifts in priorities, and the unpredictable nature of life. Rather than ending friendships prematurely, try looking at these bonds through a more compassionate lens. Recognize that personal growth doesn't follow a predictable or "one-size-fits-all" script.

Take a moment to reflect on how your friend's current priorities or limitations may differ from yours or serve purposes that you might dismiss. For instance, your constantly traveling single friend may envy the stability of your home life just as much as you might crave their adventurous freedom. Everyone's life has trade-offs, and being open to that reality can shift your perspective.

Understand that busyness, stress, or personal struggles may limit even the most caring friend's ability to show up as often as they once did. If a friend seems distant or less involved, it might not be because they don't care; they may just be managing their own challenges. It's important to recognize when your own expectations, changing ideals, or personal issues might be influencing your feelings of disappointment or judgment toward them.

Creating space for friends to express their authentic selves without fear of being judged can breathe new life into the relationship. Instead of assuming they've lost interest, offer an opportunity to have open conversations about how you both feel and what you both need. You may be surprised to find that you're both hoping to reconnect more deeply, but have hesitated because of unspoken assumptions or unexpressed concerns.

However, it's important to approach this with compassion, not demands. Don't expect perfection or future guarantees from your friendships. Instead, focus on what makes the friendship meaningful in the present moment. By being flexible and understanding, you can navigate life's twists and turns together, allowing your relationship to grow in unexpected ways.

With consistent empathy and communication, long-standing friendships can evolve and strengthen, even when life pulls you in different directions. It's in these moments of grace and understanding that you give your friendships the room they need to survive, adapt, and thrive through the ups and downs of life's journey.

Techniques to Judge Colleagues' Intentions Less Negatively

The workplace can be a breeding ground for misunderstandings. Stress, tight deadlines, competition, and limited personal connections can all contribute to negative assumptions about colleagues. It's easy to judge a co-worker's actions or motivations harshly, especially when there's a lack of personal investment or context. However, adjusting your perspective can uncover surprising empathy that improves work relationships and overall team dynamics.

Here are some techniques to help shift your workplace perspective and judge your colleagues' intentions more generously:

1. Look Beyond Surface Snapshots

It's natural to react quickly to a co-worker's abrupt tone or a blunt email, but often, those reactions are based on incomplete information. Instead of assuming bad intentions, pause and consider the bigger picture:

- Does the colleague have a particularly heavy workload this week?

- Are they going through personal challenges like illness or grief?
- Could there be external pressures you're unaware of?

When tensions arise, try asking clarifying questions to get more context before forming a judgment. Understanding the situation more fully can change how you interpret their behavior.

2. Highlight Helpful Intentions

Mistakes and oversights happen in every workplace. When they do, look beyond the immediate error and focus on the positive intent behind the action:

- Did they make a mistake while trying to contribute efficiently or take initiative?
- Were they aiming to meet a deadline, even if they missed some details?

By acknowledging their good intentions, you create a supportive environment where correction can happen without shame or resentment. This helps preserve their dignity and encourages a culture of learning rather than blame.

3. Share Vulnerability First

One way to reduce tension in the workplace is to model vulnerability. If you're open about your own uncertainties, weaknesses, or past mistakes, you invite others to drop their guard and reciprocate:

- Admit when you're unsure about a project or struggling with a task.
- Share moments when you've made errors or misjudgments.

By being honest about your own imperfections, you build trust with colleagues and foster a work culture that is more understanding and less judgmental.

4. Make Time for Personal Check-Ins

We often forget that co-workers have lives outside of work that affect their actions and behavior. Building personal connections through informal check-ins can change how you view your colleagues:

- Ask about their interests, family, or hobbies.
- Have quick chats about non-work-related topics, like their favorite sports teams or weekend plans.

This can transform work relationships from strictly professional interactions into more meaningful connections. Shared laughter and bonding over common interests create goodwill, which can soften how you interpret their actions in the workplace.

5. Turn Office Rivals into Friendly Challengers

Competition in the office can easily lead to resentment, but it doesn't have to. Reframing competitive colleagues as friendly challengers, rather than enemies, can shift your mindset:

- Instead of viewing them as trying to undermine you, see them as motivating you to do your best work.
- Instead of envying their success, use it as a learning opportunity. What can you adopt from their approach to improve your own work?
- Remember that a leadership role or opportunity may mean different things to you and a rival. Understand that each person's motivations come from unique personal or career goals.

By viewing rivals through this lens, you can turn competition into an opportunity for mutual respect and growth. Periodically asking for advice or offering compliments can build camaraderie without compromising your own drive to succeed.

6. Make Room for Missteps

Everyone has bad days, and judging someone based on isolated incidents isn't fair. If a colleague misses a deadline, seems distracted, or is unusually short-tempered, give them grace:

- Ask yourself if their behavior is part of a pattern or just a one-time occurrence.
- Consider the pressures they might be under, either at work or in their personal lives.

Approaching their missteps with empathy instead of judgment creates a more forgiving work environment. By doing so, you contribute to an atmosphere where people feel supported, not scrutinized.

7. Reframe Colleagues' Success

It's easy to feel resentful when a colleague gets a promotion, recognition, or praise for their work. However, instead of focusing on the negative emotions, use their success as inspiration:

- What strategies or habits helped them achieve their goals?
- How can you learn from their example to grow in your own role?

By reframing their success as an opportunity to learn, you shift your mindset from competition to collaboration. Let their achievements motivate you to push yourself further while maintaining your integrity and commitment to ethical work.

Loving Relationships

The New Way to Relate

In a previous section, we explored the concept of defining your world, a principle that also applies to relationships. Many people face challenges in their relationships because they struggle to understand the true purpose behind them. Without a clear understanding of what they want out of a relationship or what that relationship is supposed to bring, it becomes difficult to cultivate the meaningful connections they desire.

In this chapter, we'll dive deeper into a new way of looking at relationships, offering a fresh perspective that can help you sustain and enhance them. By uncovering the deeper purpose of relationships, we can learn how to approach them with more intentionality and insight.

The Purpose of Relationships

Relationships are a two-way street. They are meant to work *for you* and *on you*—but only if you are willing to be honest with yourself and with the other person involved. So, what is the true purpose of a relationship?

The answer is both simple and profound: the purpose of relationships is to act as mirrors, reflect our inner selves, and help us grow. They offer us opportunities for self-discovery and personal development, pushing us to become more aligned with our true selves.

Think of relationships as both a reflection and a challenge. When you interact with someone else, they mirror back aspects of your personality, beliefs, and emotional state. At the same time, they provide opportunities for growth by highlighting areas where you may need to evolve, adapt, or gain deeper understanding. This dynamic allows you to become more aware of who you are while offering a chance to refine yourself through the relationship.

The Journey Starts with You

The most crucial relationship you'll ever have is the one with yourself. It's the foundation for all other connections in your life. Without clarity about who you are, your values, and what you believe in, it becomes hard to build healthy relationships with others.

Many times, confusion and conflict in external relationships are reflections of the lack of clarity within your own self-relationship. When we are unsure of our own needs, desires, or boundaries, we project that uncertainty onto others. If we don't understand who we are or what we truly need, we enter relationships from a place of confusion, expecting the other person to fill in the blanks.

The key, then, is to clarify and strengthen your relationship with yourself first. By understanding your own beliefs, needs, and emotions, you set the groundwork for deeper, more fulfilling connections with others. You approach relationships from a place of wholeness rather than expectation, allowing the other person to complement and support your growth, rather than fulfill gaps you haven't yet acknowledged in yourself.

Reflecting for Growth

In any relationship, there will be moments when the other person challenges your assumptions, values, or actions. While these moments can be uncomfortable, they offer important opportunities for growth. When someone challenges you, it's an invitation to reflect: "What is this person reflecting back to me about myself? How can this challenge help me grow?"

Rather than viewing relationship struggles as roadblocks or failures, you can begin to see them as stepping stones for personal evolution. The more we learn from the reflections our relationships provide, the more we grow as individuals.

It's important to note that this process works both ways. Just as the people you connect with reflect aspects of yourself back to you, you also serve as a mirror for them. Every relationship is an opportunity for mutual growth, where both parties can learn from each other's strengths, weaknesses, and unique perspectives.

A New Way of Sustaining Relationships

By understanding the deeper purpose of relationships as opportunities for reflection and growth, you can sustain and enhance your connections in a more intentional way. Here are some practical steps to help build stronger relationships:

1. Self-Reflection: Regularly check in with yourself to understand your feelings, needs, and desires. Ask yourself, "What am I looking for in this relationship?" and "What can I contribute to it?"

2. Embrace Challenges: Instead of running away from conflict or discomfort, use these moments to reflect on what the relationship is revealing about you. Are there unresolved fears or insecurities that need to be addressed?

3. Be Open and Honest: Healthy relationships thrive on open communication. Be honest with both yourself and the other person about your feelings, expectations, and boundaries.

4. Support Each Other's Growth: Relationships are a two-way street. While you are growing, remember that the other person is also evolving. Encourage each other's personal growth and be patient with the process.

5. Stay Curious: Approach your relationships with curiosity rather than rigid expectations. Everyone you meet has something to teach you, and every relationship can help you learn something new about yourself.

Through His Eyes: Understanding Guy Perspectives

In this section, we'll talk about how guys often think and feel in relationships—and why some things can get tricky. Society and certain expectations don't always make it easy for men to share their emotions. But relationships grow when people understand and support each other, especially through life's ups and downs. We'll discuss simple ways to help guys open up bit by bit and explain why it's worth trying new approaches to grow closer.

The goal isn't to tell men to totally change who they are, nor to ignore the fact that vulnerability can feel uncomfortable. Instead, it's about finding healthy balances where men feel safe expressing themselves while knowing their partner will listen without judgment.

In the end, strong, caring relationships are built when both partners make space to understand where the other is coming from. As we explore the male perspective around bonding and feelings, we hope to spark acceptance and help build stronger connections.

Communicating Emotional Needs

In relationships, guys may sometimes find it tricky to express what they're feeling. It's not always about being shy, but there's often an unspoken rule that men should be tough and not show too many emotions.

Imagine you have a map, and on this map are your emotions—happiness, worries, sadness. Now, picture it being hard for guys to point at that map and say, "Hey, I'm feeling this way."

Why is it Tricky?

1. Society's Unwritten Rules: Society often says men should be like superheroes—strong, tough, and not too emotional. Expressing vulnerability can feel like breaking those rules.

2. Fear of Misunderstanding: There's also a worry that if guys share too much, their partners might not understand or might misinterpret what they're saying. So, instead of risking that, it sometimes feels easier to stay quiet.

Why It Matters:

Imagine having a favorite food but keeping it to yourself. How would your partner know to make that dish for you? It's similar in relationships. If you don't express what's on your emotional map, your partner may not know how to support you when you need it.

Simple Steps to Share:

1. Start with Small Marks on the Map: Take baby steps. Share one thing that makes you feel better or one thing that helps the relationship.

2. Use Everyday Words: Keep it simple. Just say what's on your mind. If you're happy, say "I'm happy." If you're stressed, just say that too.

3. It's Okay to Ask for Help: If expressing feelings is hard, say "I'm not sure how to explain this, but I want you to understand."

Why It's Worth the Effort:

By sharing your emotional map, you help your partner understand you better. Think of it as giving them a guide to your heart. Mutual understanding strengthens relationships. Remember, your feelings are important—they guide the direction of your life. Sharing them isn't breaking any rules; it's building a better connection.

Intimacy: Understanding the Connection

Intimacy is about more than just physical closeness. It's about feeling emotionally connected with someone and sharing your innermost feelings. Think about a close friend with whom you laugh at inside jokes or share secrets. That's intimacy—building a bond beyond just surface-level interaction.

While physical intimacy like hugging or holding hands is important, emotional, intellectual, and even spiritual intimacy matter just as much. It's about knowing each other deeply and feeling like you're in sync with one another.

Different Types of Intimacy:

1. **Emotional Intimacy:** The ability to share vulnerabilities—your joys, sadness, fears, and frustrations—and to support each other through life's challenges.

2. **Intellectual Intimacy:** Having deep conversations about shared interests or exciting ideas, creating closeness through mental engagement.

3. **Spiritual Intimacy:** Sharing your ethical values or life philosophies, deepening the bond by aligning your core beliefs.

4. **Physical Intimacy:** A non-verbal way to express affection and closeness—whether it's holding hands, hugging, or other forms of touch that show love and support.

Why Intimacy Matters:

Imagine intimacy as a treasure chest where you keep your special thoughts, dreams, and feelings. When you share this treasure with your partner, you build trust and create a safe space for mutual understanding and growth in the relationship.

How to Build Intimacy:

1. **Share Your Feelings:** Be open about your emotions.

2. **Discuss Your Interests:** Share things you both enjoy and can bond over.

3. **Respect Each Other's Beliefs:** Be open to beliefs that may be different from your own.

4. **Little Acts of Closeness:** Small, caring gestures go a long way in building intimacy.

In a Nutshell:

Intimacy isn't just one thing—it's many forms of connection that make a relationship special. By sharing more of yourself, you strengthen the bond with your partner and build a connection that lasts.

Two Reasons Men Desire Sex

1. **A Sense of Success in the Relationship:** For many men, sex is closely tied to feeling successful in a relationship. It can feel like a mental game, with the reward of intimacy being a way to celebrate the effort put into building the relationship.

2. **Reassurance of Love and Attraction:** Men often desire sex because it reassures them that their partner still loves, cherishes, and finds them attractive. It's a way to feel valued and connected.

For women, sex is often tied more closely to emotions. Their desire may ebb and flow depending on factors like stress, worries, or the emotional connection they feel. Men may see sex as a goal or a conquest, while women often need emotional alignment first to feel vulnerable enough for physical closeness.

Bridging the Gap:

Men could benefit from understanding that women often need mental and emotional connection before physical intimacy. Meanwhile, women could reassure men that physical closeness remains important in their relationship, supporting their partner's confidence.

Mutual understanding helps redefine intimacy, making it a shared experience rather than a conquest. This creates stronger, more respectful relationships where each person is valued as an individual, not just by gender roles or assumptions.

Through Her Eyes

Women are often celebrated for their remarkable ability to juggle multiple responsibilities, whether it's managing careers, households, or caregiving roles. But beneath the surface of what looks like having it all together, there's often an unseen emotional and mental toll. The constant balancing act can leave women feeling overwhelmed, tired, and isolated. In these moments, they may not be seeking quick fixes but rather support and understanding.

Consider the delicate balance of encouraging a child's independence while still offering care, or managing a parent's healthcare from afar. Add to this the challenges women face at work, where they may endure condescending comments but stay silent to maintain peace. On top of this, there's the invisible labor—organizing doctor's appointments, handling home repairs, or managing family schedules. When there is no emotional support, these burdens accumulate quietly, eventually leading to burnout.

Understanding Emotional Fatigue

For men, it's crucial to understand that mental fatigue doesn't stem from weakness but from taking on more than is humanly possible. Women may hesitate to admit they're overwhelmed, pushing past their limits in an attempt to maintain perfection.

There's no shame in acknowledging that sometimes the load becomes too much to carry alone.

Offering empathy, and being a listening ear, can often be more helpful than trying to "fix" the problem. Though practical help is important and appreciated, the act of simply being there to listen without judgment signals a deeper level of support. It shows that you're in it together, ready to face challenges as a team.

When men offer help without trying to "rescue" the situation, they allow room for joint strategies to emerge. It shifts the dynamic from "here's how I'll fix it" to "how can we work through this together?" Offering gentle encouragement to let go of less important tasks or lower perfectionist standards can also ease the mental load.

Challenges Women Face

1. **Feeling Constantly Pressured and Exhausted:** Trying to juggle multiple duties perfectly can lead to stress and strain.

2. **Downplaying Their Own Limits:** Women may push themselves too far, due to perfectionism or ignoring their own tolerance levels.

What Helps

1. **Listening Without Judgment:** Sometimes the best way to support is to simply listen. When women feel heard and appreciated, it creates space for resetting expectations and finding balance.

2. **Practical Support:** Sharing household responsibilities evenly can greatly improve relationships. However, it's important that support is offered with genuine intention and without resentment.

Responsibility is Genderless

An essential question couples should ask themselves is, *"How do you see me?"*

The way partners perceive each other plays a huge role in their interactions. Many responsibilities in a relationship get divided according to traditional gender roles, but what if we shifted the perspective? What if we looked beyond roles tied to gender and focused instead on individual abilities and strengths?

For instance, while a man cannot breastfeed, nurturing a child emotionally and physically is very much a father's role too. Similarly, just because a woman can nurture doesn't mean she can't also be the primary breadwinner. The key is that care and responsibility are not bound by biology but by capability and willingness.

In some relationships, women may earn more than men. This doesn't imply that the man is lazy or shirking responsibility. Rather, he can pursue other ways to contribute, perhaps through education, career changes, or stepping up in the household. Financial dynamics don't define a person's value or worth; what matters is how both partners work together toward shared goals.

Breaking Gender Stereotypes

It's also important to recognize that physical differences between men and women don't limit what they are capable of doing. If a woman wants to pursue a physically demanding job, she should be encouraged to do so. Similarly, if a man excels at managing household tasks, he shouldn't feel restricted by societal norms.

Ultimately, relationships thrive when people work together based on individual strengths, not assumptions about gender roles. Society shouldn't dictate who does what based on gender stereotypes. **Sharing responsibilities based on personal strengths**—rather than pre-assigned roles—often leads to greater harmony and mutual respect.

Overcoming Relationship Shadows in New Bonds

In the delicate realm of love, our past relationships often cast shadows that quietly influence new connections. Whether those shadows take the form of heartbreaks, old habits, or misplaced optimism, they affect how we perceive and engage with fresh beginnings. Let's explore the different perspectives people have when it comes to carrying past emotional baggage into new relationships, and how gently shifting those perspectives can lead to healing and growth without imposing a rigid "right" way of thinking.

Different Perspectives on Past Relationships

1. The Ghosts of Heartbreak Past

Some individuals carry their past heartbreaks with them like heavy, silent companions. The emotional scars from past relationships act as a filter, coloring their view of new connections. While these people long for new beginnings, their past pains often overshadow the possibilities for fresh love, causing them to hesitate or fear getting hurt again.

2. The Eternal Optimist

At the other extreme is the eternal optimist. They brush off past relationship hurts as minor bumps on the road, believing that each new relationship is untainted by the past. They compartmentalize emotions and assume they can start fresh without considering how unresolved feelings might still influence their behavior or reactions.

3. The Cautious Explorer

Some approach new relationships like cautious explorers, aware of their past wounds but hopeful for a better future. They recognize that their emotional scars have shaped them, and though optimistic, they remain guarded. Their caution stems from a need to heal, yet they also realize that growth requires some risk.

4. The Unwitting Saboteur

Then there are those who, without meaning to, allow past relationship patterns to sabotage their new bonds. These individuals have absorbed behavior patterns from previous experiences—perhaps mistrust, avoidance, or emotional withdrawal—that subtly dictate how they navigate new relationships, often hindering true connection without them even realizing it.

Shifting Perspectives for Healthier Bonds

Moving past relationship shadows isn't about forgetting the past or pretending the pain never happened. It's about transforming those experiences into opportunities for growth and self-discovery. Here's how each perspective can evolve into something more empowering:

1. From Ghosts of Heartbreak to Resilient Learner

For those who feel haunted by past heartbreaks, healing involves shifting from seeing emotional scars as wounds to viewing them as signs of resilience. Each hurtful experience can be seen as a lesson, making them stronger and more compassionate. In this way, the pain of the past is no longer something to fear but rather a source of wisdom that can guide them in building healthier, more fulfilling connections.

2. From Eternal Optimist to Compassionate Realist

The eternal optimist can benefit from grounding their boundless hope in compassionate realism. By acknowledging that past relationships have shaped their emotional landscape, they can approach new relationships with more awareness. This doesn't mean giving up their optimism, but rather recognizing that healing from the past and learning from it makes their hope for the future even stronger and more meaningful.

3. From Cautious Explorer to Intentional Healer

For the cautious explorer, the journey forward involves embracing intentional healing. Rather than simply guarding themselves against potential heartbreak, they can take active steps toward self-discovery and emotional growth. This could involve seeking therapy, journaling, or engaging in deep self-reflection. The goal is to build a stronger emotional foundation, allowing them to approach new love with confidence and openness, rather than fear.

4. From Unwitting Saboteur to Mindful Transformer

The unwitting saboteur can begin transforming their approach by becoming more mindful of how past behaviors are influencing their current relationships. This requires self-awareness—identifying patterns and making conscious choices to act differently. By actively choosing new behaviors and letting go of old habits, they can break free from the past's constraints, allowing new relationships to blossom without the weight of unresolved issue.

Transforming Shadows into Strength

Navigating the influence of past relationships on new ones is a process of self-rediscovery and growth. It's not about erasing the past but about transforming it into a source of strength. The shadows of past hurts do not need to haunt us forever. Instead, they can guide us toward new perspectives, deeper understanding, and more meaningful connections.

By accepting that our past experiences shape us—but don't define us—we empower ourselves to approach new relationships with wisdom and an open heart. We learn to let go of fear, embrace healing, and allow love to flourish again, with each step forward a testament to the resilience of the human spirit.

Every relationship is an opportunity to grow, learn, and love in new ways. By acknowledging the lessons of the past and adjusting our perspectives, we create space for healthier, more authentic connections. Through resilience, compassion, and mindfulness, we can weave new stories of love—ones that honor our pasts while embracing the limitless possibilities of the future.

The Journey of Love: Navigating Love Languages, Expectations, and Expressing Needs

In the intricate dance of relationships, understanding love languages, managing expectations, and expressing needs is much like learning a heartfelt language that is unique to each person. Each relationship is a delicate interplay between these components, and how we view them can significantly shape the depth and fulfillment we experience. Let's explore the diverse perspectives people bring to this profound subject and look at subtle, compassionate ways to shift these perspectives without imposing a single narrative or limiting view.

Different Perspectives on Love

1. The Hopeless Romantic

For the hopeless romantic, love is often expressed through grand gestures and passionate declarations. This perspective values deep emotional connection and sweeping expressions of affection, with expectations set high. There is a desire for an all-encompassing love, one that transcends the ordinary and speaks to a fairy-tale ideal.

2. The Pragmatist

The pragmatist views love as something to be expressed through tangible actions, responsibility, and commitment. Love is grounded in practical, day-to-day acts that ensure stability. Expectations focus on the importance of consistency, fulfilling roles, and maintaining an organized and efficient partnership. Pragmatists often see expressing needs as a straightforward exchange where practical solutions are key.

3. The Communicator

For communicators, love is spoken in words and understood through dialogue. Open, honest, and transparent conversations are their love language, and they expect the same level of engagement from their partner. Needs are expressed verbally, and mutual understanding is crucial. For the communicator, the key to a successful relationship lies in the constant exchange of feelings, thoughts, and concerns.

4. The Protector

The protector shows love through acts of service, safeguarding their partner's well-being. Their love language revolves around actions that provide a sense of security, stability, and care. Expectations are rooted in being the dependable one who handles situations, offering protection and reassurance. Expressing needs for the protector may feel more natural when conveyed through action rather than words, as they value doing over saying.

Shifting Perspectives on Love Languages

Just as relationships evolve, so too can our perspectives on love languages, expectations, and how we express our needs. A shift in perspective doesn't erase our natural tendencies but expands our capacity to honor and understand the ways love can be expressed. Here's how each of these perspectives can transform for greater harmony:

1. From Hopeless Romantic to Balanced Appreciator

For the hopeless romantic, learning to appreciate the beauty in smaller, consistent gestures of love can be a game-changer. While grand expressions of love are cherished, recognizing that depth can also reside in the everyday—whether it's a quiet hug, a simple compliment, or doing something kind without fanfare—broadens the scope of meaningful connection. Balance between romance and practicality makes love more sustainable.

2. From Pragmatist to Emotionally Connected Realist

The pragmatist, who often values actions over words, can expand their view of love by embracing emotional connection as a necessary complement to practicality. While handling daily responsibilities is important, adding emotional warmth and vulnerability into the mix deepens intimacy. Love is multi-faceted, and bringing more emotional awareness into pragmatic routines enriches both partners' experience of the relationship.

3. From Communicator to Mindful Listener

For the communicator, shifting from a focus on expression to active listening can create a richer bond. Listening for non-verbal cues and understanding what remains unspoken can sometimes say more than words. Developing the ability to "hear" emotions behind actions, silences, or body language offers an expanded sense of connection. It's not just about being heard—it's about offering a space where both partners feel deeply understood.

4. From Protector to Vulnerable Partner

For protectors, opening up to vulnerability can feel counterintuitive, but it's essential for deeper intimacy. Often, protectors give their love through actions but may struggle with asking for emotional support themselves. Understanding that being vulnerable doesn't diminish strength, but rather enhances trust and connection, allows them to share their inner world with their partner. Expressing needs becomes a way to build a more balanced relationship where both partners can rely on each other emotionally.

Cultivating Love Through Mutual Understanding

As individuals navigate their own love languages, expectations, and ways of expressing needs, they contribute to a constantly evolving relationship landscape. This isn't about steering anyone toward a rigid understanding of how love "should" work, but rather encouraging an ongoing journey of mutual understanding, acceptance, and growth.

Here are a few ways to encourage this evolution:

1. Respect Individual Love Languages

A key to success is recognizing that everyone has their own way of giving and receiving love. What feels natural to one partner may not come as easily to the other. Take the time to learn your partner's love language and find ways to honor it. Whether it's through physical touch, words of affirmation, acts of service, or quality time, each expression of love has its own value and deserves to be acknowledged.

2. Adjust Expectations Thoughtfully

Understanding that your partner's needs and expressions of love may differ from your own allows you to release rigid expectations. Relationships thrive on flexibility, and by adjusting your mindset to be more open and inclusive, you allow both partners to express themselves authentically.

3. Create a Safe Space for Needs

Part of a healthy relationship is creating a space where both partners can express their needs without fear of judgment. This means fostering an environment of trust, where vulnerabilities are met with compassion rather than critique. By gently encouraging open dialogue about emotional, physical, and mental needs, partners can feel supported as they navigate life together.

4. Celebrate Growth, Not Perfection

Remember, relationships are not about perfection but progress. Embrace the idea that both partners are growing—sometimes at different rates and in different directions. Celebrate small victories, like finding new ways to support each other, instead of focusing on what may still need improvement.

Attachment Styles and Emotional Patterns

In relationships, the way we connect—or pull away—often stems from invisible threads woven in our earliest experiences. These emotional patterns, known as attachment styles, quietly guide how we love, seek comfort, or guard our hearts. Understanding these subtle yet powerful forces can unlock deeper intimacy and more authentic connections.

The Clinger

Imagine someone standing on the edge of a cliff, constantly reaching out for reassurance, terrified the ground beneath them will give way. The Clinger craves closeness as if it's the only thing keeping them safe from a freefall. Their emotional security is tethered tightly to their partner's attention—each missed call or delayed text feels like a crack in their foundation. To them, love is like a lifeline, vital and consuming. But what if that lifeline slackens? The fear of abandonment gnaws at them, pulling them deeper into a cycle of neediness, even as they long for stability and fulfillment.

The Avoider

On the other side of the spectrum is the Avoider, someone who moves through life like a lone wolf, savoring their independence. They hold space between themselves and others, cherishing their personal freedom above all. To the Avoider, deep emotional bonds are not an anchor but a weight. Intimacy is something to sidestep, a possible trap that might confine them, smother them. So, they keep their distance, retreating into their inner world when emotions start running high, believing autonomy is the only way to stay whole.

The Anxious

Then, there's the Anxious. Picture someone teetering between wanting to be held and fearing the embrace might not last. They dance in a state of perpetual uncertainty, one foot always ready to run, but the other rooted in their longing for connection. In their heart, attachment is a bittersweet experience—comfort and unease braided together. One moment, they're leaning in, craving closeness, but the next, they're pulling back, consumed by the fear that the love they've found will slip through their fingers. Their world is colored by the worry of 'too much' or 'not enough,' leaving them in a delicate, exhausting balance.

The Secure

And then, there's the Secure. They stand with an open heart, unafraid of love's demands or its gifts. To them, attachment is neither a trap nor a crutch, but a natural exchange—a flowing river where intimacy and independence can coexist in harmony. Their emotional landscape is vast, unclouded by fear of abandonment or entrapment. They trust the strength of their bonds, knowing they are flexible enough to withstand both distance and closeness. In their world, love is a steady flame—nurtured, but never suffocating. For them, relationships are spaces of growth and safety, and their emotional patterns bend and stretch as needed, always in service of the connection.

Shifting Perspectives

Just as the seasons shift, so too can our attachment styles evolve if we're willing to reflect and grow. The journey from fear-based patterns to secure connections isn't about abandoning who we are but expanding into a fuller, more balanced version of ourselves.

From Clinger to Secure

For the Clinger, transformation begins when they learn to stand firm on their own two feet. It's not about rejecting love, but realizing it's something to share, not cling to. Imagine them as a tree, once uprooted and desperate for stability, now growing deep roots of self-assurance. Instead of seeking constant validation, they start to nurture an inner belief that they are enough, just as they are. In this newfound strength, love is no longer a lifeline—it's a shared dance, where both partners stand on solid ground.

From Avoider to Secure

The Avoider's journey is one of stepping out from the shadows, letting the warmth of connection touch them without fear of losing themselves. They begin to understand that love doesn't have to suffocate—it can breathe. Picture them once behind a thick wall, now cracking open a window, letting just enough light in to see that intimacy doesn't mean loss of freedom, but the gain of richness. Slowly, they come to see that personal space and shared moments can coexist without erasing one another.

From Anxious to Secure

For the Anxious, peace comes not from clinging or retreating but from quieting the storm within. Imagine someone who has spent their life on edge, finally stepping onto solid ground. They start to realize that love is not something to be earned through vigilance, but something they deserve inherently. Their self-worth no longer hinges on the other person's response, and the constant fear of rejection fades as they cultivate love within. With each step, they learn that true security begins not with their partner, but with themselves.

Attachment styles, like rivers, can be redirected, and emotional patterns can be rewoven into new narratives. Each shift, each small revelation, opens up a wider, more harmonious way to connect with ourselves and those we love. The key is not to judge where we start but to embrace the possibility of change.

By understanding these patterns and leaning into the wisdom of growth, we can turn the tides in our relationships. Whether Clinger, Avoider, Anxious, or Secure, each of us can shape our story into one where love is both freeing and grounding—a journey of becoming more fully ourselves while building bridges to others.

Turning Conflicts into Growth

Relationships, like the sea, aren't always calm. Storms can brew in the form of arguments, and when the waves get choppy, we're faced with a choice: navigate through them together or risk being pulled apart by the current. Everyone has their own way of dealing with conflict, from those who see arguments as dealbreakers to those who see them as valuable opportunities for growth. Let's dive into these perspectives and explore how we can transform conflicts into stepping stones toward deeper connection.

Different Ways People See Arguments

1. The Dealbreaker Believer:

For some, arguments are like flashing red lights, signaling that something in the relationship is fundamentally wrong. They fear that disagreements are cracks in the foundation, warning that the relationship may not last. Each fight feels like a step closer to the end, and the focus shifts to worry and doubt rather than resolution.

2. The Avoider:

The Avoider would rather smooth things over than face the discomfort of confrontation. To them, harmony is more important than hashing things out, even if it means swallowing their true feelings. Avoiders often believe that peace is better than progress, but over time, unresolved issues can create a silent distance that's hard to bridge.

3. The Fighter:

For the Fighter, arguments are about winning. The focus is on proving a point, and sometimes, it's easy to lose sight of the relationship in the heat of the battle. Emotions run high, and the need to be right overshadows the need to understand. While Fighters may feel a temporary victory, the aftermath can leave emotional bruises that take time to heal.

4. The Learner:

Then, there are those who see conflict as a chance to understand one another better. For the Learner, disagreements are not roadblocks but opportunities. They approach arguments with a sense of curiosity, asking, "What can I learn from this?" For them, conflicts hold the potential to deepen intimacy and foster personal growth.

How to Change Your View

Turning conflict into growth requires a shift in how we perceive disagreements. Rather than seeing them as moments of division, we can learn to view them as invitations to strengthen our bond.

1. From Dealbreaker Believer to Curious Explorer:

If you're someone who tends to view arguments as dealbreakers, try adopting the mindset of a curious explorer. Instead of fearing that every disagreement spells the end, see it as a door to deeper understanding. What's really at the heart of the issue? What are both of you trying to express, but perhaps not communicating clearly? Approach conflicts with curiosity, and you may uncover new layers of your relationship that strengthen your connection.

2. From Avoider to Brave Communicator:

If you're used to avoiding conflict to keep the peace, becoming a brave communicator can open new pathways for intimacy. It's scary to speak up, especially when you fear rocking the boat. But honesty builds trust, and expressing your needs, even when it feels uncomfortable, can lead to a stronger, more authentic bond. By bravely voicing your feelings, you're not just protecting the relationship; you're nurturing it.

3. From Fighter to Team Player:

If you tend to view arguments as battles to be won, try shifting your focus to teamwork. In a healthy relationship, it's not about one person coming out on top—it's about working together to find solutions. Instead of seeing your partner as an opponent, see them as your teammate. Together, you can tackle the problem and grow stronger for it.

4. From Learner to Thoughtful Navigator:

If you already see arguments as opportunities to learn, you're on a great path. But there's always room to evolve. Become a thoughtful navigator by choosing the right time and place to address sensitive issues. Some conflicts are best tackled when emotions are calm. Approach each disagreement with the intent to grow not just individually, but as a couple. Be intentional about how and when you address challenges, ensuring that each conversation helps both of you move forward.

Embracing Conflict as a Catalyst for Growth

It's natural to want smooth sailing in relationships, but the reality is that storms will come. The trick isn't to avoid the waves or fight against them but to learn to navigate through them together. When we stop seeing conflicts as threats and start viewing them as opportunities for growth, we can transform how we communicate, connect, and collaborate with our partners.

Turning conflicts into growth is about creating a space where both individuals feel heard, respected, and valued—even when they disagree. It's about shifting the focus from winning or losing to understanding and evolving. Every argument, when approached with an open heart, can become a stepping stone toward a stronger relationship, a chance to reveal deeper truths about ourselves, and a way to build resilience together.

So the next time you find yourself in the middle of a disagreement, pause. Ask yourself: What can I learn from this? How can we use this moment to grow, not just as individuals but as a team? In doing so, you'll discover that every storm holds the potential for clearer skies and deeper love.

Unlocking the Secrets to a Lasting Relationship

In relationships, initial attraction may draw two people together, but it's the deeper mental and emotional connection that sustains the bond. While physical appearance may catch the eye, it's the intellectual and emotional connection that holds the heart over time. Here are some key pillars that support a lasting, meaningful partnership:

1. Clear Communication as the Bedrock

Healthy relationships rest on the foundation of open and honest communication. To sustain a relationship, both partners need to express their thoughts, feelings, and desires clearly, without fear of judgment. Equally important is listening—truly hearing your partner's perspective and understanding what's beneath their words. This exchange fosters mutual understanding and trust, allowing the relationship to flourish.

In the early stages of a relationship, communication tends to be easier, driven by excitement and discovery. But as the relationship matures, maintaining that same level of openness becomes vital. When both partners feel heard and valued, conflicts can be navigated with empathy, and misunderstandings can become opportunities for growth.

2. Supportive Bonds that Strengthen

A lasting relationship isn't just about being there for each other when things are tough—it's about building each other up, celebrating victories, and sharing in each other's successes. The bond between partners should be one where each person feels uplifted and supported. When life throws challenges your way, having a partner who believes in you and encourages your growth makes all the difference.

True support also means providing space for your partner to evolve. Instead of holding on to fixed ideas of who they "should" be, encourage their personal growth and exploration. Whether it's supporting a new hobby, career aspiration, or personal development, being each other's biggest cheerleader strengthens the foundation of the relationship.

3. Allowing Growth through Reflection

Expectations can sometimes stifle the natural flow of a relationship. Instead of forcing a partner to fit into a mold or preconceived ideas, give them the room to grow and evolve. By encouraging self-reflection and self-expression, both partners can thrive as individuals within the relationship.

Relationships should be seen as a journey of growth, where each partner evolves in their own right while contributing to the shared experience. When both individuals are allowed to change and develop over time, the relationship becomes a dynamic, ever-evolving bond rather than a stagnant one stuck in past versions of yourselves.

4. Understanding Deep Beliefs

As the initial excitement of a new relationship settles, it's easy to start noticing your partner's quirks, habits, or traits that may irritate you. But often, it's not your partner's behaviors themselves that create distance—it's the stories and assumptions we create around them.

When you begin to interpret every small disagreement as a sign that your partner doesn't care or every mistake as evidence that they aren't right for you, the real issue lies not in the relationship, but in the negative narratives you're telling yourself. Instead of seeing your partner as someone who holds you back, recognize that they can be a mirror, reflecting aspects of yourself you need to work on.

The key to long-term success in a relationship is understanding the core beliefs and values that drive each partner. What motivates your partner's decisions? What experiences shaped their views on life, love, and relationships? By exploring these deeper layers, you create a sense of empathy and understanding that strengthens the emotional connection.

True freedom in love comes when you let go of rigid expectations and embrace the reality of who your partner truly is. Rather than holding onto an idealized version of what you want them to be, you allow yourself to see the full complexity of their personhood. When both partners operate from a place of compassion—for themselves and each other—the relationship can grow in unexpected and fulfilling ways.

Putting These Principles into Practice

Understanding and applying these four principles—**Clear Communication, Supportive Bonds, Allowing Growth, and Understanding Deep Beliefs**—lays the groundwork for a healthy, lasting relationship. But let's dive deeper into one principle: **Understanding Deep Beliefs**, as it often holds the key to resolving long-standing conflicts.

Imagine that over time, your partner's habits begin to wear on you. Maybe they leave the dishes undone or forget to call when they're running late. These small annoyances start to overshadow their positive traits—the kindness they've always shown, their sense of humor that once charmed you, or their willingness to be there for you in tough times. As these small irritations build up, you start creating a narrative: "Maybe they don't care about the relationship. Maybe I deserve better."

This is where understanding deep beliefs comes in. It's easy to project your frustrations onto your partner, blaming them for why you feel unfulfilled or disconnected. But more often than not, the source of these feelings lies within you. Perhaps it's your belief that being loved means having every need perfectly met. Or maybe it's your fear of vulnerability, causing you to misinterpret their actions as a lack of care.

The wake-up call comes when you realize that by blaming your partner, you're avoiding the real work—confronting your own limiting beliefs and insecurities. Freedom comes when you recognize that love doesn't fit neatly into expectations. Instead of holding onto a mental checklist of how your partner should behave, you can open yourself to their true essence, flaws and all. In doing so, you create space for authentic connection, where both partners feel safe to be their full selves.

The Power of Letting Go of Narratives

By releasing negative narratives and expectations, you start to appreciate your partner for who they truly are, not who you think they should be. Differences, rather than being points of contention, become opportunities for growth and understanding. The key to sustaining love lies not in perfection, but in acceptance and curiosity.

With compassion for yourself and your partner, the relationship flourishes. You move away from the mindset of fixing or controlling and step into a space of shared exploration, where love can expand and deepen with time.

Allowing Growth Through Reflections

In relationships, there's a rare magic that happens when someone truly sees you—not just the persona you project to the world but the raw, unfiltered essence of who you are. When intimacy deepens, we become vulnerable in ways we never expected, sometimes revealing parts of ourselves we've long ignored. And sometimes, those revelations are uncomfortable.

I remember when my wife first began offering insights into my inner world, picking up on struggles I hadn't even fully acknowledged in myself. At first, I resisted. Her observations felt too sharp, too close to insecurities I'd spent years avoiding. But as our relationship deepened, and as trust became the bedrock of our connection, I realized her feedback wasn't an attack—it was a gift.

In many ways, she became a mirror. Not the kind you check to see if your tie is straight, but the kind that shows you your blind spots—those hidden corners of your soul you tend to overlook. She reflected back to me the parts of myself that needed attention, not out of judgment, but out of love. This reflection revealed insecurities, unchecked habits, and even beliefs that weren't serving me anymore.

Instead of shrinking away from these truths, I chose to embrace them. I began to ask myself the tough questions: **Why does this trigger me? Why am I holding onto this insecurity?** These weren't easy questions, and the answers weren't always comfortable. But through this process, I found growth.

It's not about perfection, but progress. My wife's perspective helped me integrate the parts of myself I had fragmented or denied, transforming those scattered pieces into a more whole and aware self.

This kind of growth requires compassion—both for yourself and your partner. Relationships, when rooted in trust and mutual respect, become sacred spaces for healing. They allow us to become more complete, not through the absence of flaws, but through the acceptance of them. So when your partner reflects something challenging back to you, try to remember that this is where true growth happens. It's not always easy, but wholeness comes through radical self-honesty.

Supportive Bonds That Strengthen

A strong relationship isn't just about weathering the storms together; it's about being an active source of encouragement for each other. There's something transformative about knowing that no matter what, you have someone in your corner cheering you on. That kind of support doesn't just build trust—it builds resilience, both individually and as a couple.

Support goes beyond helping each other through the hard times. It's also about celebrating the wins together, no matter how small. It's about being genuinely invested in each other's success, not in a competitive way but from a place of genuine love. By creating a bond where both partners uplift one another, you make the relationship stronger. You help each other become better versions of yourselves, not by molding or controlling, but by encouraging self-expression and growth.

Clear Communication: The Bedrock of Relationships

Communication isn't just a means to get your point across—it's the art of building understanding, fostering connection, and bridging the gap between two individuals. It's what keeps a relationship strong and evolving. The way we communicate can either create harmony or cause discord, and the foundation of lasting communication is clarity and authenticity.

When both partners can express themselves openly and honestly, a powerful synergy is created. But communication isn't just about talking—it's about listening. And that's where the real art comes in.

Active Listening

Listening is a skill we often take for granted. How many times have you found yourself nodding along while your partner speaks, but your mind is elsewhere, already crafting a response? In that moment, you've lost the connection. True listening requires full presence.

The magic of active listening lies in your ability to engage without the compulsion to fix or solve. It's not about inserting your thoughts or finding solutions—it's about being fully immersed in what the other person is saying, allowing them to be heard in the purest sense. Think of it as a meditative practice where your partner's words become your sole focus. It deepens the connection and enriches your relationship in ways that surface-level conversations can't.

Let's break down **three styles of listening**:

1. Listening to Encourage

- **Purpose:** To uplift and support your partner.
- **Caution**: Be mindful that encouragement doesn't overshadow genuine understanding.

2. Listening to Relate

- **Approach:** Finding common ground through shared experiences.
- **Caution:** Avoid making the conversation all about you; steer clear of hijacking the dialogue to relate everything back to your own stories.

3. Effortless Listening

- **Challenge:** This is the hardest but most powerful form of listening.
- **Practice:** Just sit, absorb, and let your partner's words wash over you without needing to respond.

Here are a few tips to master effortless listening:

- Imagine yourself as a tree stump—solid, grounded, and simply absorbing without judgment.
- Picture your partner as a wise mentor, allowing their words to flow into you, ready to be taken in without interruption.

When you truly listen, you create a space for deeper connection, which in turn builds trust and intimacy. By cultivating this ability, not only will you improve your relationship with your partner, but you'll also strengthen your connection to your own inner wisdom. Listening, in its truest form, is an act of love.

Allow yourselves to be each other's mirrors, guiding one another toward the truest versions of yourselves. Listen deeply, support fully, and grow endlessly together.

The Art of "I" Statements: A Path to Healthier Communication

In the world of communication, how we express ourselves can be the difference between creating connection or conflict. One powerful tool to foster understanding is the use of "I" statements. This technique involves speaking from your own perspective—articulating your thoughts, feelings, or concerns—rather than casting blame or making accusations. The result? More honest, respectful, and constructive dialogue.

Let's break down how using "I" statements works, with examples of how this approach can transform communication in various scenarios:

1. Expressing Feelings:

- **Typical approach:** "You never listen to me."
- **"I" statement:** "I feel unheard when I share something and it doesn't seem like you're paying attention."

Why it works: The first approach accuses the other person of a specific behavior, which often triggers defensiveness. The "I" statement, on the other hand, is about your emotional experience. It invites the other person to understand how their actions impact you, fostering empathy rather than defensiveness.

2. Addressing Issues:

- **Typical approach:** "You always leave your things lying around."
- **"I" statement**: "I get frustrated when I see things left out because I feel responsible for cleaning up."

Why it works: Instead of pointing the finger and escalating the situation, the "I" statement highlights your feelings and the reason behind them. It opens the door for a constructive conversation about shared responsibilities rather than turning it into a blame game.

3. Sharing Concerns:

- **Typical approach:** "You are so careless with money."
- **"I" statement:** "I feel anxious when I think about our finances because I worry about saving for the future."

Why it works: The first statement sounds accusatory, which can put the other person on the defensive. By framing it with an "I" statement, you're expressing your concerns about a shared issue without shaming the other person, making it easier for both of you to find a solution together.

4. Avoiding Accusations:

- **Typical approach:** "You're not supportive."
- **"I" statement:** "I feel unsupported when I'm dealing with stress and need a little more reassurance or help."

Why it works: This approach avoids characterizing the other person as unsupportive and instead highlights your emotional needs. It invites the other person to engage in the conversation with a mindset of helping rather than defending themselves from criticism.

5. Taking Responsibility for Emotions:

- **Typical approach:** "You make me so angry."
- **"I" statement:** "I get angry when we argue because I feel like I'm not being heard."

Why it works: Instead of blaming the other person for "making" you feel a certain way, the "I" statement takes responsibility for your own emotions. It acknowledges the role that your feelings play in the situation, promoting a discussion that's rooted in understanding rather than blame.

Why "I" Statements Matter

At the core of "I" statements is the idea of taking ownership of your own feelings and reactions. This approach encourages thoughtful dialogue rather than defensive exchanges. When we speak in "you" statements—"you never," "you always," "you make me"—we're more likely to trigger defensiveness in the other person. In contrast, "I" statements open up space for both people to feel heard and respected.

- **Less Blame, More Understanding:** "I" statements remove the accusatory tone from conversations, making it easier for both parties to stay calm and engage in the conversation without feeling attacked.
- **Encouraging Empathy:** By expressing your feelings and needs without judgment, you invite the other person to empathize with your experience rather than immediately go on the defensive.

Promoting Self-Awareness: Using "I" statements requires you to pause, reflect on your feelings, and identify what's truly bothering you. This self-awareness leads to more meaningful and thoughtful interactions.

Tips for Mastering "I" Statements:

- **Start with Emotion:** Reflect on how you're feeling before you respond to a situation. Whether it's frustration, sadness, or anxiety, identify the emotion behind your reaction.
- **Be Clear and Specific:** When using an "I" statement, avoid generalizations. Instead of "You never listen," specify the behavior that triggers your feelings: "I feel unheard when I'm talking and you're checking your phone."
- **Keep It Constructive:** After stating your feelings, suggest a way forward. For example, "I would feel more appreciated if we could set aside time to talk without distractions."

Love: It's Not What You Think

Choosing to Love vs. Deciding to Love

When we think about love and relationships, one key question arises: do we **choose** to love, or do we **decide** to love? While these two words might seem interchangeable, they carry very different meanings that can profoundly affect the course of our relationships.

Choosing to love suggests that love is a flexible, day-to-day decision, influenced by emotions, circumstances, and how we feel in the moment. It implies that love is conditional, subject to shifting moods and changing conditions. When love is a choice, it can be fickle—here one day, gone the next. While this mindset might be appropriate for casual dating or exploring the early stages of a relationship, it often lacks the deep-rooted stability needed for enduring love.

On the other hand, **deciding to love** carries much more weight. To decide to love someone is to make a deliberate, conscious commitment—a promise that transcends the whims of daily emotion. When we **decide** to love, we're not simply reacting to how we feel in any given moment. Instead, we're making a binding declaration to stand by our partner through thick and thin. It's a steadfast vow to make them the central focus of our affection, even when things get tough.

Deciding to love brings a sense of permanence and resilience to the relationship. While emotions may fluctuate, the decision to love remains firm, providing a solid foundation built on trust, loyalty, and enduring commitment. This kind of love offers strength and stability, even when faced with challenges, doubts, or difficult times.

Choosing love can be momentary and fleeting, but deciding to love is transformative—it reflects a deeper level of devotion that strengthens the bond over time. By embracing the power of deciding to love, we elevate our relationships from fragile and reactive to enduring and unbreakable. It's in this commitment that we find true connection, one that reaches the depths of our souls and offers lasting solace and strength.

Love Wants to Be Expressed

Love is not something scarce or difficult to find; it's a wellspring within each of us, constantly ready to flow outward. But often, we don't allow love to flow freely because of internal blockages that we've built up over time.

The Two Main Blockages:

1. **Past hurts or negative beliefs:** Emotional wounds from previous relationships, or growing up without healthy examples of love, can lead us to believe that love is hard to come by. These experiences create barriers that prevent us from fully giving or receiving love.

2. **The search for perfection:** We often place conditions on love, believing that it can only be real if we find the "perfect" partner. This keeps us stuck, waiting for an ideal that may never come, instead of realizing that love is an expansive energy

within us that can embrace real, imperfect, but valuable connections.

By identifying these blockages, we can open the gates for love to flow freely once again. The key to letting love flourish is realizing that love doesn't come from someone else—it's something we generate within ourselves.

Making Love Flourish:

We can unleash the power of love by:

1. **Being present with love:** Spend time simply feeling love for yourself, for others, or for life itself without focusing on getting love in return. This practice creates an unconditional love that doesn't depend on approval or reciprocation.

2. **Engaging in spiritual practices:** Use tools like meditation, mantras, or affirmations to cultivate and send love outward. When we practice love without expecting anything in return, we build a momentum of love that keeps growing.

3. **Seeing relationships as learning opportunities:** Instead of looking to relationships to fill a void or heal our insecurities, view them as chances to grow in understanding and compassion. Your partner isn't there to save you but to reflect your strengths and weaknesses so you can grow together.

With regular practice, love stops being something we chase or wait for—it becomes an energy we nurture within ourselves, a force we can give, share, receive, and renew. We start to see love as something infinite, not tied to conditions, but flowing from our very being.

As the poet Rumi so beautifully said, "*Your task is not to seek for love, but merely to seek and find all the barriers within yourself that you have built against it.*" When we dismantle these inner barriers, we unlock an endless well of love, allowing it to pour out and nourish the people, relationships, and experiences around us.

The Takeaway

Love is not just something we stumble upon or find—it's something we actively create and choose to nurture. While choosing to love can feel fleeting, **deciding to love** provides the stability and commitment necessary for enduring relationships. And by recognizing and removing the internal barriers that block our ability to love fully, we tap into an infinite well of love that enriches every aspect of our lives.

When we understand that love isn't something we get from others, but something that naturally flows from within us, we stop chasing perfect relationships and start building meaningful, grounded connections. We stop measuring love in grand gestures or fleeting emotions and begin to appreciate its steady, quiet presence in everyday moments.

Ultimately, love is about creating a space within ourselves that is open, free, and capable of embracing both the beauty and the imperfection of those around us. By choosing to **decide** to love and letting go of the barriers that keep love at bay, we create a deeper, more fulfilling experience of life and relationships—one rooted in compassion, understanding, and unwavering commitment.

Navigating Love's Ups and Downs

In relationships, it's natural for feelings to shift over time. When we're in love, we easily focus on our partner's best qualities, but when those feelings fade, we may fixate on their flaws instead. Our thoughts are deeply influenced by how we feel—when we're in a negative space, those thoughts can create emotional distance between us and our partner.

Falling out of love can feel like losing the spark that once connected us. It's confusing and sometimes overwhelming as doubts begin to cloud our thoughts. But here's the truth: love isn't gone forever; it's just waiting to be rekindled. By understanding that our beliefs and emotions shape our thoughts, we can begin to challenge those negative thinking patterns.

Through compassion and understanding, we can rebuild the connection we thought was lost.

Love is like a game, with moments of being "in bounds" and "out of bounds." Imagine you and your spouse playing together on the "football field of love." When negative thoughts and feelings get in the way, it's like stepping out of bounds—you're temporarily disconnected. But just because you've stepped out doesn't mean the game is over. You can always find your way back to love, reconnecting with your partner by coming "back in bounds."

The key to staying in love—or finding your way back—is **forgiveness**. Forgiveness is a powerful remedy for falling out of love because it helps clear the emotional clutter of the past, giving you both a fresh start. When you hold onto grudges, you carry a weight that only breeds more unhappiness. But when you forgive, you free yourself from that burden and allow your relationship to grow once more.

Forgiveness isn't about condoning hurtful actions. It's about recognizing the humanity in the other person—their ignorance, their mistakes—and understanding that we all falter sometimes. As T.D. Jakes wisely said, *"Unforgiveness is like drinking poison and waiting for the other person to die. Let it go!"* Holding onto anger or resentment doesn't serve you; it only prolongs the distance. Conflicts will happen, but true strength comes from being able to forgive, let go, and move forward without bitterness.

Trust, like love, is always present. You're always trusting in something—whether it's a positive or negative outcome. Often, we place our trust entirely in other people, which can lead to disappointment because people are unpredictable and imperfect. Instead, try trusting in something greater—whether that's God, the universe, or whatever higher power you believe in—to guide you toward the best outcome.

Trusting in people to behave in certain ways sets you up for frustration. But **trusting that people will show you who they truly are** allows you to make informed decisions. In other words, don't expect someone to conform to your idea of how they should act. Instead, trust that they will be themselves, and from there, you can decide if and how you want to engage with them.

When you shift your focus from controlling others to trusting in the process, you free yourself from unnecessary stress. **Trust that things will work out for your highest good**, even if the road feels rocky. What you see and experience is meant to help you grow and learn. By trusting in the bigger picture, you can adjust your perspective and make decisions from a place of clarity.

In the journey of love, **feelings will change**—that's just a natural part of the ride. But falling out of love doesn't mean the journey is over. It's an opportunity to rediscover your connection by practicing forgiveness, learning to trust, and being open to healing past wounds.

By embracing these moments of uncertainty with compassion, you give your relationship a chance to evolve, grow, and become even stronger. Love isn't static; it moves, shifts, and changes with us. And when we understand that, we can ride the waves of love's ups and downs with grace, knowing that the heart of love is always within reach, waiting to be rekindled.

Key Takeaways

1. **Purpose of Relationships:** Relationships are meant to help us grow and become more of ourselves. Their purpose is to provide opportunities for reflection and personal development.
2. **Relationship Appreciation:** Letting go of unrealistic romantic expectations shaped by myths and movies allows us to better appreciate and support real partners.
3. **Transforming Friendships:** Transforming lifeless friendships requires honest reflection, adventurous questions, complementary collaboration on shared passions, and small caring gestures.
4. **Improving Work Relationships:** Workplace relationships improve when we extend generous interpretations about colleagues' intentions, look beyond surface impressions, highlight helpful motives, share vulnerability first, and make time for personal check-ins.

Love That Last: The journey of lasting love involves effective communication, standing by each other during challenges, celebrating successes together, understanding deep beliefs driving behaviors, embracing all facets of ourselves and partners with compassion, and turning conflicts into opportunities to grow intimacy.

Chapter 7

Shifting Your Professional Lens

"If you desire to make a difference in the world, you must be different from the world." **-Elaine S. Dalton**

Viewing Work through an Empowering Lens

For many people, work can feel like a daily grind—a means to pay the bills and sustain life outside of the job. But what if we changed our perspective and viewed work as something more meaningful? When we adjust how we see work, we open ourselves to the possibilities of purpose, impact, and connection. Rather than seeing your career as just a paycheck, what if you viewed it as a way to contribute positively to the world, build relationships, and grow your talents?

Start by examining what truly matters to you. What are your values, passions, and vision for contributing to the world? Once you're clear on that, you can proactively shape your work to reflect your inner compass, instead of passively accepting the status quo. You may discover opportunities for fulfillment and growth that were hiding in plain sight, simply because you weren't looking for them.

Your coworkers are not just nameless faces that you tolerate while counting down the minutes to quitting time. They, too, have dreams, challenges, and gifts that you may not yet have noticed. When you approach work with curiosity and empathy, asking about your colleagues' aspirations and sharing in small joys, you build human connection. Shared laughter makes the workday lighter. When you lead with warmth, the invisible walls between cubicles fall.

Lasting fulfillment doesn't come from fancy titles or corner offices. It springs from within, through the satisfaction of small daily accomplishments that align with your values and aspirations. There are lessons to be learned even in failure, and growth often happens at a slow, steady pace. When you align your internal compass with your external work, you'll find that every task, no matter how small, contributes to something bigger.

Stay mindful that every project you complete and every interaction you have is part of a larger ripple effect, subtly shaping the world around you. Striving for excellence and compassion in your work creates positive energy that spreads to others. When you view the tasks on your to-do list as pieces of a bigger puzzle, you'll realize that you're not just working for yourself—you're helping to build a community.

As the poet Khalil Gibran wrote, *"You work so that you may keep pace with the earth and the soul of the earth."* In that spirit, see your professional life not as an obligation but as a canvas for love-fueled creation. Through this empowering lens, work becomes an opportunity to better the world and feed your soul.

The Power of "Get To" in Professional Life

In our fast-paced professional lives, the language we use can have a profound impact on our mindset and how we perform. Two simple words—"get to"—have the power to transform the way we approach our daily tasks and obligations.

How often do you say things like, "**I have to finish this project**," or "**I have to attend this meeting**," or even "**I have to take my kids to practice**"? These phrases, while common, carry an underlying sense of obligation and sometimes even complaint. What if, instead, we shifted our mindset by replacing "have to" with "get to"?

When you say, "**I get to finish this project**," or "**I get to go to work today,**" you're inviting gratitude into your mindset. These words acknowledge the privilege of having meaningful work when so many are still searching for employment. They shift your focus from a sense of duty to a sense of opportunity. Suddenly, work becomes something you're fortunate to do, not something you have to endure.

Even in life's mundane moments, like driving through traffic or attending routine meetings, saying **"I get to"** reminds us that we are fortunate to have these opportunities, especially when many others do not. For instance, **"I get to drive in traffic,"** becomes a recognition that you have the freedom and ability to travel, a blessing many others don't have.

In professional settings, it's easy to fall into the trap of thinking we have no choice but to fulfill our responsibilities. But the truth is, we always have a choice in how we approach those responsibilities. Our attitudes are in our control. When we view each task as a chance to learn, grow, or make a difference, we unlock more meaning and satisfaction in our work life.

Acknowledging that life is a gift, not an obligation, changes everything. Even when challenges arise, approaching them with gratitude can turn difficult situations into opportunities for growth and learning. The mindset of *"I get to"* allows us to see each professional opportunity as a privilege rather than a burden.

Instead of thinking of our careers as something we have to endure, let's collectively decide to approach them as gifts. By recognizing the opportunities we "get to" engage in each day, we invite purpose and gratitude into our lives. When we change the way we speak about work, we change the way we experience it. So, let's declare that every day is an opportunity, not a chore. Let's embrace each moment of our professional journey, knowing that we "get to" live this life and make the most of it.

Focus for a Change

In the pursuit of success, focus stands as the guiding light for great achievers. Tony Robbins famously said, *"Where focus goes, energy flows."* When we look at icons like Oprah Winfrey, Harrison Ford, and Dr. Seuss, one thing becomes clear: their ability to concentrate on mastering one thing was a key factor in their extraordinary accomplishments. These individuals harnessed the power of focus, pouring their energy into their craft, which led to remarkable results.

Dan Henry, a successful online marketer with an 8-figure business, shares a similar insight in his book *Digital Millionaire Secrets*. He discusses the concept of the "circle of focus" and highlights the pitfalls of juggling too many pursuits at once. Henry explains that when he spread his attention too thin across multiple projects, his sales dropped significantly. This taught him the importance of focusing on one key area at a time, a lesson many entrepreneurs and achievers come to realize.

I experienced a similar wake-up call in my own journey. When I first started writing this book, my attention was scattered across multiple interests—designing the book cover, podcasting, public speaking, and even exploring opportunities in television and film. I felt busy, constantly moving from one task to another, but the book's progress was slow. People around me started noticing, questioning why the book was taking so long. I realized that while I was doing a lot, I wasn't making significant progress on any one thing. The phrase *"jack of all trades, master of none"* echoed in my mind.

The challenge of divided attention is something many of us face. We often try to juggle numerous projects, thinking that being busy means being productive. But in reality, splitting our focus across too many pursuits leaves our main goal neglected. In my case, I was busy but not making real progress, because I wasn't focusing on the book the way I needed to.

The turning point came when I made a conscious decision to streamline my focus. I decided to cut back on other pursuits and channel my energy into finishing the book. It wasn't easy at first—there's always the temptation to say yes to every new opportunity—but it became clear that by trying to do everything, I was moving nowhere fast.

The lesson I learned is simple yet profound: to achieve meaningful results, we must focus our energy on one thing at a time. When we scatter our attention across too many activities, our progress slows down. But when we concentrate on mastering one area, our energy becomes more powerful, and success follows.

The Difficulty Behind Focus

In today's fast-paced world, staying focused can be challenging. Distractions are everywhere, procrastination creeps in, and prioritizing tasks can feel overwhelming. To understand why focus is difficult, let's dive into three key reasons: *distractions*, **procrastination, and lack of prioritization.**

Reason #1: Distractions

In a world full of distractions, it's no surprise that staying focused can be tough. From constant phone notifications to the allure of social media, our attention is frequently pulled in different directions.

Ways Distractions Happen:

- **Phones Are Everywhere:** Our smartphones are incredibly useful but can quickly lead us from work to entertainment in a single swipe.

- **Social Media Pulls Us In:** Social media platforms are designed to be engaging, with notifications that prompt us to stop what we're doing and check updates.
- **Too Much Information:** We're bombarded with information from news sites, social media, emails, and more. This can overwhelm our brains, making it harder to focus on one thing deeply.

Why It Matters:

Distractions don't just interrupt our work; they also prevent us from thinking deeply. Jumping from one thing to another makes it hard to solve problems or come up with creative solutions. When our attention is scattered, our productivity and creativity suffer.

Dealing with Distractions:

- No Tech Zones: Designate specific times or areas where you don't use electronic devices. This helps create an environment that's free from interruptions.
- Planned Breaks: Schedule breaks to check messages or social media. This prevents them from constantly disrupting your workflow.
- Focus Apps: Use apps that block distracting websites and help you stay on task.

- **Mindfulness Techniques:** Practices like mindfulness meditation can improve your ability to control your attention. This helps you return your focus to the task when distractions pop up.

By understanding how distractions sneak in and using strategies to manage them, you can regain control over your focus.

Reason #2: Procrastination

Procrastination, or delaying tasks until later, is something we all deal with. But delaying important tasks can lead to stress and anxiety, especially when deadlines are looming.

How Procrastination Happens:

- **Lack of Motivation:** Sometimes tasks seem dull or too difficult, making it hard to get started.
- **Fear of Failure**: The fear of not doing something perfectly can cause us to avoid the task altogether. It's easier to put it off than to face potential failure.
- **Big Picture Overwhelm**: When a task seems too large, it can feel overwhelming. This makes us more likely to delay starting because we don't know where to begin.

Why It Matters:

Procrastination creates unnecessary stress, leads to rushed and poor-quality work, and can even make us feel guilty or anxious about not completing tasks on time. It becomes a cycle that feeds into more procrastination.

Dealing with Procrastination:

- Set Small Goals: Break down big tasks into smaller, more manageable parts. Achieving these small goals can make the larger task feel less overwhelming.
- Find Motivation: Connect the task to something you care about. Understanding why a task is important to you can help boost your motivation.
- Set Deadlines: Even if a task doesn't have a strict deadline, create one for yourself. This adds a sense of urgency and helps you stay on track.
- Reward Yourself: Plan small rewards for completing tasks. This can create a positive association with getting things done.
- Start Anyway: Often, the hardest part is starting. Even if you don't feel motivated, begin the task, and you might find it easier to continue once you've started.

By tackling procrastination head-on, we can reduce stress and create a more productive workflow.

Reason #3: Lack of Prioritization

When everything seems urgent or important, it becomes difficult to decide where to start. Without clear priorities, it's easy to feel overwhelmed, which makes it harder to focus.

How Lack of Prioritization Happens:

- **Equal Weight to Everything:** Treating all tasks as equally important makes it hard to decide where to begin. This lack of clarity can result in inefficiency.
- **Focusing on Urgency, Not Importance**: Some tasks may seem urgent but aren't crucial for long-term goals. It's essential to distinguish between what's urgent and what's truly important.
- **Not Considering Deadlines:** Ignoring deadlines or being unaware of them can contribute to poor prioritization. If you don't know when something is due, it's harder to prioritize it properly.

Why It Matters:

Without proper prioritization, we may spend too much time on less important tasks, leaving the critical ones incomplete. This leads to unmet deadlines, stress, and a sense of not accomplishing meaningful goals.

Dealing with Lack of Prioritization:

- **Create To-Do Lists:** List all your tasks, then rank them based on importance and deadlines. This gives you a clear roadmap for what to focus on first.
- **Identify High-Impact Tasks:** Focus on tasks that contribute most to your long-term goals or overall success.
- **Set Realistic Deadlines**: Establish deadlines for each task, keeping in mind its urgency and importance. This keeps you on track.
- **Learn to Say No:** If you're overwhelmed, don't be afraid to say no to additional tasks. It's essential to manage your workload.
- **Use Time Management Techniques:** Tools like the Eisenhower Matrix help categorize tasks based on their urgency and importance. This can help you make smarter decisions about where to invest your time.

By prioritizing effectively, you can improve focus and productivity, ensuring your energy is directed towards what truly matter.

Why Focus is Important in Professional Life

Focus plays a crucial role in our professional lives. Here's why it matters:

- **Achieving Goals:** When we focus on a specific goal, we can dedicate our time and energy to it, making it more likely that we'll achieve it. By eliminating distractions, we make steady progress.
- **Enhancing Performance:** Focus enhances our ability to absorb information, make better decisions, and perform at a higher level. Concentrating on the task at hand improves overall efficiency.
- **Reducing Stress:** Staying focused on the present moment helps reduce mental clutter, lowering stress and anxiety. Letting go of worries about the future or regrets about the past allows us to cultivate a sense of calm and clarity.

Focus and Motivation:

Motivation, at its core, operates on a simple yet profound principle: the drive to seek pleasure while avoiding pain. This dynamic guides our choices, actions, and even inaction across different areas of life. Whether in love, career, or creativity, our motivation hinges on this delicate balance between pursuing fulfillment and avoiding discomfort.

In every major decision, whether it's about relationships, professional pursuits, or creative expression, motivation involves a complex dance between what we desire (pleasure) and what we fear (pain). To make meaningful progress in any area of life, the pleasure we seek must outweigh the pain we fear. Recognizing and understanding these inner calculations is the first step toward mastering our focus and motivation.

Let's explore three common scenarios that highlight this balancing act in action:

1. The Love Dilemma: Balancing Connection and Fear of Loneliness

In the realm of love and relationships, the motivation to find meaningful connections is a powerful force. However, it often exists alongside the fear of heartbreak, rejection, or loneliness. This tug-of-war between longing for love and the dread of emotional pain can cause many to settle for unfulfilling relationships or avoid deeper connections altogether.

- **Seeking:** Connection, romance, and shared fulfillment.
- **Avoiding:** Loneliness, rejection, and the potential pain of separation.

For someone yearning for love, the desire to experience closeness and joy with another person is deeply motivating. Yet, the fear of being vulnerable—of potentially getting hurt—can create a protective barrier. The comfort of staying single or remaining in a lukewarm relationship may seem like a safer bet than risking emotional pain for the chance of something deeper.

How to Reframe This Dilemma:

Understanding that love, like anything meaningful, involves risk can help shift the balance. Rather than focusing on the fear of what could go wrong, we can choose to focus on the potential for personal growth, connection, and joy that comes with taking emotional risks. Love requires vulnerability, and recognizing that this vulnerability is not weakness but courage can be a powerful motivator to take that leap.

2. The Professional Crossroads: Navigating Passion and Fear of Instability

In the professional world, many people find themselves stuck between pursuing their passion and staying in a safe, secure job that doesn't bring fulfillment. The motivation to pursue meaningful work is often outweighed by the fear of financial instability or failure, leaving many to settle for a career that doesn't excite or inspire them.

- **Seeking:** Passion, purpose, and a dream career.
- **Avoiding**: Financial risk, uncertainty, and instability.

Here, the pain of financial insecurity can overshadow the desire for career fulfillment. The idea of leaving a stable job to pursue something more meaningful may seem like too big a risk, even if the current job feels like a grind. It's easy to stay in the comfort zone of predictability rather than face the discomfort of the unknown.

How to Reframe This Crossroads:

Rather than focusing solely on the risk, take a more balanced view of the potential rewards of pursuing your passion. Career shifts don't always have to happen overnight. Start with small steps—explore your passion in your free time, build skills on the side, or slowly transition into your dream field. Viewing the journey as a gradual evolution rather than an all-or-nothing leap can make the goal feel more achievable.

3. The Creative Conundrum: Balancing Self-Expression and Fear of Criticism

For those in creative fields, such as writers, artists, or musicians, the desire to share their unique gifts with the world often clashes with the fear of criticism, failure, or rejection. The deep motivation to create is sometimes paralyzed by the fear of judgment, and the idea of risking financial instability in a competitive field adds another layer of hesitation.

- **Seeking:** Self-expression and sharing one's gifts with the world.
- **Avoiding:** Criticism, failure, and financial instability.

In this case, the fear of putting oneself out there creatively—opening up to the judgment of others—can feel overwhelming. The desire to protect oneself from the potential pain of rejection can stifle the creative impulse, leaving many artists or creators stuck in a cycle of hesitation and self-doubt.

How to Reframe This Conundrum:

Reframe the act of creating as an act of courage, not perfection. Remember, everyone who puts their work out into the world faces criticism at some point. Rather than seeing criticism as a reflection of failure, view it as a step toward growth. Creativity is about expression and exploration, not about pleasing everyone. Allow yourself to embrace the uncertainty and focus on the joy of the process rather than the outcome.

Mastering Motivation's Machinery

The formula of motivation—seeking pleasure while avoiding pain—is at the heart of every decision we make. Whether in love, career, or creativity, the key to moving forward is ensuring that the potential for fulfillment outweighs the fear of discomfort or risk. When we get stuck in patterns of inaction or stagnation, it's often because we're prioritizing present comforts (however limited) over the potential for future growth. We're letting the fear of pain dictate our actions instead of focusing on the pleasure of reaching our goals.

The solution lies in recognizing these inner calculations and recalibrating our focus. Ask yourself: **What do I stand to gain?** Shift attention toward the pleasure and growth awaiting on the other side of discomfort, and you'll find the courage to move beyond fear. Whether it's pursuing love, taking a leap in your career, or expressing yourself creatively, trust that the journey—while challenging—holds immense potential for fulfillment.

By mastering this delicate balance, you can unlock the true power of focus and motivation, propelling you forward toward the life you truly desire.

The Inner Race: Outdo Yourself, Not Others

In life, a common myth insists that success is about beating others—being the best student, the top athlete, or the one who climbs the corporate ladder faster than everyone else. It's a deeply ingrained narrative, one that pushes us to believe that the only way to be happy or successful is by outshining others. But as research and lived experience show, this isn't the path to real fulfillment. True success doesn't come from defeating external competitors but from an ongoing commitment to outdoing ourselves.

Motivation: The Power of Self-Improvement

The key to long-term happiness and success lies in shifting our focus inward, competing not with others but with ourselves. While external recognition might bring short-lived satisfaction, genuine joy comes from personal growth and inner fulfillment. Consider children immersed in play or artists lost in their craft—not for external praise, but for the sheer pleasure of creation. This kind of internal motivation, rooted in passion, leads to deeper contentment and often greater professional success.

When we stop chasing validation from others and start cultivating an inner drive, we begin to appreciate our unique gifts. Like snowflakes, no two individuals share the same exact story, strengths, or perspectives. Sculptor Fredrik Raddum's reflection that "The lotus flower blooms most beautifully from the deepest and thickest mud" reminds us that our struggles and vulnerabilities often fuel our greatest growth. The challenges we face and the lessons we learn along the way become the foundation for our success.

Outdoing Yourself: A Journey of Self-Expansion

When we define success by how far we've come—by outpacing our past limitations—something remarkable happens. Instead of measuring our worth against others, we focus on how we can improve, learn, and grow. There's no final finish line, only continuous opportunities to unlock new talents, gain deeper insights, and develop courage. In this ongoing inner race, we become the heroes of our own story, constantly leveling up as we strive toward our highest potential.

Of course, self-competition must have healthy boundaries. Setting unrealistic expectations for ourselves can lead to frustration and burnout. The key is finding a balance: holding high aspirations while being compassionate with ourselves through setbacks. Patience, humor, and self-kindness are essential to making this journey sustainable. Growth accelerates not when we're hard on ourselves, but when we embrace the process, focusing on the thrill of progress instead of dwelling on what went wrong.

Freeing Yourself from External Validation

One of the most profound shifts in perspective comes when we stop seeking validation from others. The more we measure our success by external standards—how we rank compared to others, how much money or fame we accumulate—the more disconnected we become from our inner joy. True peace and fulfillment come when we live from the inside out, focusing on our own growth rather than constantly checking how we measure up to others.

This mindset transforms our sense of competition. Instead of running a race against illusions—against people who have their own journeys and challenges—we realize our only competitor is the person we were yesterday. Every step we take toward becoming a better version of ourselves is a victory. In this sacred space of personal growth, success isn't about reaching a specific destination; it's about the journey itself.

The Inner Race Mentality: Stories of Success

Countless individuals who have reached great heights did so not by focusing on beating others, but by relentlessly working to improve themselves. They shifted from feeling like failures to becoming victors, from struggling to thriving, all by focusing on personal development and adding value to the world. By mastering the art of self-competition, they reached levels of success that others might only dream of, not because they outshone others, but because they consistently outperformed their past selves.

This "inner race" mentality—this drive to constantly outdo who you were yesterday—sustains high achievement. Each time you push past yesterday's limits, you uncover new abilities, new goals, and new heights to reach. The race never ends, but that's the beauty of it. As you grow, so does your vision of what's possible. And with every step, you get closer to unlocking the person you were always meant to become.

Embracing the Endless Climb

This journey of self-improvement has no final lap. There is no ultimate "finish line" in life where you can declare that you've won. Instead, the goal is constant, joyful progress. Each stage of growth prepares you for the next, helping you become more in tune with your true potential. The path may not always be easy, but with each new skill you develop, with each new challenge you overcome, you move closer to realizing your fullest self.

The beauty of the inner race is that it's yours alone. You set the pace, the goals, and the vision. And in doing so, you free yourself from the pressure of keeping up with others. Instead, you get to revel in the excitement of seeing just how far you can go—how much more you can become—by focusing on your unique gifts and embracing every part of your journey.

Victory Lies Within

The myth of success as a competition with others is exactly that—a myth. Real, lasting success comes from the quiet, steady pursuit of outdoing yourself, day by day, challenge by challenge. It comes from turning inward, understanding that your journey is yours alone, and recognizing that the real victory lies in becoming the best version of yourself.

With each step, you'll discover new talents, unlock hidden reservoirs of strength, and outpace the limits you once thought defined you. And as you continue on this path, you'll realize that success is not a fleeting moment or an external validation—it's the fulfillment of knowing you've grown, evolved, and reached new heights on your own terms.

So run your own race. Compete not against others, but against the person you were yesterday. In doing so, you'll find not only success, but joy, purpose, and lasting fulfillment. And that, truly, is the greatest victory of all.

Key Takeaways

1. **Work with Purpose:** Find meaning and connection in your career by aligning it with your values and passions. Mold your work to reflect your inner compass.
2. **Build Genuine Relationships:** Connect with colleagues by showing interest in their aspirations. Break barriers through shared laughter and warmth, recognizing the strengths of others.
3. **Focus on Inner Fulfillment:** Seek contentment through daily accomplishments aligned with your goals. Embrace failures as learning opportunities and understand that true fulfillment comes from within, not external status.
4. **Make a Positive Impact:** Be mindful of how your work contributes to the wider world—complete tasks with excellence and compassion, recognizing their role in building community.

Create with Purpose: View your profession as an opportunity for meaningful creation. Align your work with a sense of purpose and recognize the chance for self-expression and contribution.

Chapter 8

Putting Together the Pieces: When Perspectives Become Reality

"Inner work is the effort by which we gain awareness of the deeper layers of consciousness within us and move toward integration of the total self." – **Robert A. Johnson**

Creating New Realities

We've explored how thoughts and feelings shape our perception of life, but the bigger question is: **How do we translate this inner world into our lived reality?** While shifting perspectives is powerful, it's action that brings these changes into the tangible world. Without action, wisdom remains abstract, hovering in the realm of ideas but never truly making an impact. **Transformation happens when we move from thinking to doing.**

At the heart of this journey lies a call to turn our internal shifts into bold actions that match our beliefs and desired outcomes.

Here are three critical elements that help us bridge the gap between our thoughts and the reality we create.

1. Making A Decision

Transformation begins with **a firm decision**—one that aligns with the expansive vision you have for your life. But commitment often requires courage, especially in the face of uncertainty. The question is: Can you step beyond doubt and trust the new possibilities your beliefs have been nurturing?

- **Growth thrives on bold decisions.** When we declare, "I am ready for this," we set the wheels of change in motion. It's in this act of claiming who we want to be that potential becomes reality. **Bold statements like "I am successful," "I am healthy," "I am creating my dream life"** are not just words. They plant seeds in the fertile soil of your subconscious mind, and, with unwavering trust, they grow into tangible outcomes.

2. Trusting the Unseen Forces

Even when we can't see concrete evidence, **there are unseen forces working in our favor** when we align our intentions with trust. This requires leaping forward with the belief that invisible currents gather beneath us, supporting our journey. It's a kind of faith that transcends logic—the faith that somewhere between the idea and its manifestation lies a mystery beyond our control.

Navigating the unknown demands that we shed the weight of doubt and **trust that the destination is near**, even if we can't yet see it. As we move forward, the veil slowly lifts, revealing the land we've been aiming for. Vindication comes when we realize that **our heart sensed truths long before we could confirm them with our minds**. There is a wisdom in letting go of disbelief and trusting that what we've envisioned is already on its way to us, guided by a force greater than ourselves.

3. Acting As If

The whispers of your heart can become **powerful voices**, and small sparks can ignite into **thunderous storms** of change. To follow your dreams, you must **act as if** they are already real. This doesn't mean pretending or forcing, but embodying the energy of your dreams, showing up in ways that reflect the future you desire.

Action solidifies transformation. Entrepreneurs who stay focused on success through tough times and people who pursue their passions with unwavering belief are acting "as if." This bridges the gap between the dream and reality, making what once seemed far-fetched feel real and attainable. Every action, no matter how small, reinforces the reality you are creating.

Wisdom lies in recognizing life's subtle nudges. The universe often gives us gentle hints that push us toward growth—whether it's an opportunity, a challenge, or an intuitive nudge. By consistently acting on these prompts, you invite your dreams into existence.

Life is a mixture of desire, trust, and action. When aligned, these three elements work together to transform your dreams into reality. Words, like seeds, shape your world. Just as a garden needs nurturing to flourish, so too does your inner world. What talents are waiting within you, ready to be shared with the world? The gifts you hold inside are not just meant for you; they are meant to uplift, inspire, and empower others.

The world is ready for what you have to offer. Are you ready to step into the bold future your dreams have been whispering about? Take the leap, trust the unseen forces, and act as if your vision is already your reality. Because, in truth, it already is.

Facing Your Inner Doubts

Meet Jada, a woman with a heart full of dreams, who longed to create a nonprofit to help children unlock their potential through art. She wasn't driven by personal fame or recognition, but by a quiet desire to nurture the hidden talents of kids overlooked by society. Yet, every time she inched closer to making her dream real, those familiar voices of self-doubt would echo, "Who do you think you are?" Even though she seemed outwardly successful, these inner doubts kept her tethered to safe jobs where her soul felt small, and her creativity suffocated.

Fear of failure, fear of looking foolish—these invisible barriers stopped Jada from fully stepping into her purpose. Years passed, and she found herself stuck, choosing comfort over passion, ignoring the strong pull inside her. But then, something shook her world. A health crisis—sudden, unexpected—made Jada face her own mortality. For the first time, she realized that the security she had clung to meant little if it cost her the purpose she was meant to live. Security, she realized, was an illusion if it kept her from the vibrant, meaningful life she knew she was called to.

In those quiet moments of reflection, Jada confronted her limiting beliefs. She heard the lies she had lived with for so long: the false comfort that playing it safe was better than the risk of failure. But now, playing it safe felt like a slow death. What kind of safety is that, she wondered, if it meant burying her dreams? With a surge of newfound courage, Jada made a bold declaration to herself and the world:

"Through me, kids will discover their greatness. My life will shine a healing light to help them shine. I will boldly show the future I want to see!"

That single, powerful affirmation was like a match striking the dark—igniting a fire in Jada's heart that had long been dormant.

It wasn't just a statement; it was a vow, a reclamation of her own strength. With that, the floodgates opened. Inspiration poured in, and her vision turned into action. She began to share her dream with others, and soon, resources and support flowed in from places she had never imagined. As the kids in her program started to flourish, Jada's resilience grew. The setbacks that once might have derailed her now only sharpened her focus. Her dream, which had once been stifled by doubt, was now lifting her, and others, higher than she ever thought possible.

Jada's story teaches us that our inner doubts, though isolating, are not insurmountable. The moment we step forward with courage, we discover that we are not alone. We find support in the most unexpected places. Our dreams have the power to soar if we give them wings—and boldness is the wind beneath those wings. What dream is waiting within you? What world do you carry inside, ready to be spoken into existence?

Creating Well-being

When Juan was diagnosed with diabetes, fear set in. He feared the disease would take over, leading him to a life of slow decline. But Juan wasn't one to accept a fate of helplessness. Instead of feeling like a victim of his diagnosis, he made a powerful decision—he would take charge of his health, mind, and spirit.

Juan dove into learning about the mind-body connection, about how thoughts and beliefs could influence physical well-being. Armed with this new understanding, he set clear and powerful goals. He wrote a statement that he repeated daily: "**I will be completely healthy by my next check-up.**" This statement became like a seed planted deep in his subconscious, one that slowly began to grow into a reality.

But it wasn't just the words—Juan paired his intention with action. He didn't dwell on what could go wrong. Instead, he began to **imagine himself fully healed**, envisioning a future where he wasn't just living with diabetes but thriving beyond it. He saw himself teaching others about the power of self-care and the mind-body connection, helping them reclaim their own health. These visions made him feel stronger, more motivated, and hopeful.

With a practical plan in hand, Santiago adjusted his diet and incorporated exercise into his daily routine. He joined a supportive community of people on similar journeys, and he kept track of his progress in a journal. **Day by day, the path to well-being became clearer.**

Even when symptoms lingered, Juan didn't waver. He acted **as if** he was already healed, embodying the healthy person he envisioned in his mind. And over time, his body followed. At his next check-up, his doctor delivered the news—his diabetes was in full remission.

Juan's journey shows us that **the power to heal and thrive** lies within us. It's not just about the physical steps we take, but the beliefs and visions we hold for ourselves. His story is a reminder that even in the face of life's greatest challenges, we can rise above them by turning belief into action. The strength we find today can become our new normal tomorrow.

The seed of human potential **wants to grow**—it is calling out for courage, action, and belief. What will you grow into? What greatness lies dormant in your heart, waiting for you to turn belief into reality?

Trusting the Process

Chasing our dreams can feel like venturing into unknown territory, leaving behind the familiar paths and stepping into a world shaped by the visions we hold in our hearts. We often get caught up in trying to map out every step, plotting how to reach that distant castle we've imagined. But here's the truth: we don't need to know every detail of the journey. We don't have to solve the "how" at every turn. The path reveals itself step by step, and our job is simply to keep moving forward with faith.

Imagine yourself as a traveler guided by a quiet inner compass, trusting the whispers of intuition and inspiration. In this journey, you may glimpse possibilities in the distance, hear the call of something greater urging you onward. You don't need to know exactly how you'll get there. Instead, trust that each step you take is bringing you closer to the outcome meant for you—even if it unfolds differently than you initially envisioned.

This is the essence of trusting the process. It means surrendering control of the specific "how" and trusting that a higher power is working with you, aligning circumstances in ways you might never predict. The journey may lead you through twists and turns, through challenges and unexpected detours, but each part of it serves a purpose. Often, what seems like a diversion is really preparing you, refining you, or leading you to something even better than you'd planned.

The beauty of trusting the process is that it frees you from the weight of constant worry. When you release the need to control every outcome, you allow yourself to experience life more fully, with openness and curiosity. You still hold the vision of what you want, but you're not rigidly attached to a single path or outcome. Instead, you trust that whatever unfolds is guiding you toward your purpose in the best possible way.

So, let go of the need to see the whole map. Walk forward with confidence, knowing that as you trust the journey, the right opportunities, people, and answers will appear. This is the art of living by faith rather than fear—embracing each step as it comes, knowing you are supported, and letting a higher power handle the details.

Applying the Wisdom of Trusting the Process

How can we take this wisdom and apply it to our daily lives? Here are some practical ways to embrace this mindset:

1. Release the Need to Control Every Detail: Stop overthinking and trying to plan out every step. Trust that as you take action, the next steps will unfold naturally. Let go of micromanaging the journey and focus on moving forward with intention and openness.

2. Hold Your Vision Loosely: It's important to have a goal in mind, but allow room for flexibility. Sometimes the journey will surprise you, leading to outcomes even better than you imagined. Embrace these shifts as part of the process.

3. See Setbacks as Redirection: Obstacles aren't always barriers; they can be stepping stones guiding you to something better. When things don't go as planned, trust that there's a reason. Look for the lesson or the new direction being offered.

4. Have Faith in a Higher Power: Whether you call it God, the Universe, or simply the flow of life, trust that a greater force is orchestrating your path. This faith allows you to surrender control and walk with a sense of peace, knowing you are supported.

5. Stay Open to Unexpected Opportunities: When you stop trying to control every outcome, you open yourself up to possibilities you might never have considered. Embrace the mystery of the journey and welcome the unexpected gifts that come your way.

By trusting the process, you free yourself from the illusion of limitations and find peace in the journey itself. Let go of the worry over "how" things will happen, and instead, embrace the adventure of "what could be." When you trust the journey, you allow life to surprise you, leading you to places beyond your imagination.

Act As If

Rosa had always known she was meant for acting, but after years of auditions that went nowhere, doubt began creeping in. **Survival fears set in.** Would she have to settle for a safer job? Was her dream slipping away?

Then Rosa remembered stories of actors who rewrote their mental scripts—people who "**acted as if**" they already had their big break long before it came. What if she tried the same? What if she started living her dream life now, acting as though she was already a working actor?

She committed to the practice immediately. **Every day became a performance of her envisioned future.** She took more theater classes, held meetings with imaginary agents guiding her career, and even drafted acceptance speeches for the award shows she was sure she'd attend. When financial fears surfaced, she replaced them with faith, knowing her talent would reveal her purpose in time.

And soon enough, her persistence paid off. **Within a few months, Rosa landed a career-launching role.** The agents who had once passed her by now saw her in a new light—a dedicated, disciplined actress who was a leading lady waiting to be discovered. By acting as if her future success was already a reality, Rosa began to shape the perceptions of directors and casting agents long before her breakthrough role. She **became the actress of her dreams** through sheer belief and action.

Similarly, Allan, a new teacher in an underfunded district, faced overwhelming odds. His students were grappling with extreme poverty, learning barriers, and societal neglect. Many of his colleagues had written off the potential of these children, but Allan made a vow to himself: **he would act as if success was assured** for each of his students.

He envisioned every child in his classroom as a future leader, innovator, and agent of change. His lessons were tailored not for struggling learners, but for **emerging thought leaders.** He wrote loving, personalized notes on their essays, imagining how these same students would one day share their talents with the world. Class discussions didn't dwell on their current hardships but instead explored **genius-level solutions to social injustices.**

Two decades later, many of Allan's former students are leading nonprofits, heading companies, and speaking at international conferences. They credit Mr. Allan's unwavering belief in them—his **"acting as if" success was inevitable**—for inspiring them to rise above their circumstances. His trust in their potential created a **bridge from dream to reality**, both for himself and his students.

In both Rosa's and Allan's stories, the common thread is this: **Acting "as if" the future they desired was already true**. They didn't just hope for success—they embodied it, day by day, action by action. In doing so, they drew the future toward them, making it tangible, real, and inevitable.

Lessons from Acting "As If"

Here's how you can apply the "Act as if" principle in your own life:

1. Commit to Your Vision: Whether it's a career goal, personal dream, or life transformation, live today **as though your dream is already real**. Take actions that align with the future version of yourself.

2. Rewire Your Mind: Create mental rehearsals where you see yourself already succeeding. Visualize the outcomes you want and **embed those images in your subconscious.** Brain scans show this kind of practice can change your neural pathways.

3. Take Bold, Consistent Steps: Even if fear or doubt tries to creep in, **keep acting as if success is inevitable.** Rosa kept auditioning, and Allan kept teaching with unwavering belief in his students. **Persistence bridges the gap** between imagination and reality.

4. Trust the Process: There's power in aligning your thoughts, actions, and beliefs. Even if the results aren't immediate, trust that every small step is bringing you closer to your destination. By acting as if the life you desire is already here, you awaken **new possibilities. Your mindset shapes your reality**, and soon enough, the world will respond to the version of you that you've dared to live out loud.

So, what reality are you ready to create? **Take the leap. Act as if.** And watch the magic unfold.

Things to Remember: Mental Conversations with Yourself

Life is, at its core, an ongoing dialogue—an elaborate series of **internal conversations** where we serve as both the speaker and the listener. Within the chambers of our minds, we constantly engage in a quiet yet profound act: persuading, negotiating, and guiding ourselves. **The way we talk to ourselves holds enormous power**, perhaps more than any external force.

When faced with choices, challenges, or even simple daily decisions, we run through this inner dialogue: weighing the pros and cons, imagining outcomes, and talking ourselves toward certain attitudes and actions. It's this quiet, internal negotiation that **steers the direction of our lives**—either toward growth and fulfillment or away from our highest potentials.

One truth always stands: **You're either talking yourself into something or talking yourself out of it**. Each moment, we choose between progress and hesitation, courage and fear, faith and doubt.

These conversations, however, don't just float on the surface. Our **subconscious mind** often carries old fears, doubts, and limiting beliefs that have quietly taken root over the years. These deep-seated whispers can undermine even our boldest aspirations. **Active, conscious self-communication** is required to either dispel those doubts or inadvertently allow them to shape our lives.

For example, when you're standing at the edge of a big decision—whether it's a career change, a new relationship, or any other leap into the unknown—your mental narrative determines your next step. Do you trust yourself enough to jump, or do you shrink back into the comfortable and familiar? In this inner battleground, where **confidence does battle with self-imposed limits**, we negotiate what we deem possible and what we do not. The **stories we repeat to ourselves**—often in whispers, sometimes in shouts—form deep grooves that direct how we show up in the outer world.

Here's the secret: **By bringing conscious awareness to this inner dialogue, you can mindfully foster positive and intentional conversations with yourself.** It means noticing when limiting beliefs arise, catching yourself in the act of self-doubt, and making a deliberate choice to shift the narrative.

Instead of letting old fears control the conversation, you can interrupt the flow of negative thoughts and **redirect them toward something expansive, hopeful, and bold.**

The Power of Inner Negotiation

Life unfolds through an endless sequence of **mental conversations**—an intimate, back-and-forth dialogue that never really stops. In this private theater of the mind, we play both roles, the **passionate speaker** and the **active listener**, in every scene.

Here's how it works:

The voice of **fear** might whisper, *"Are you sure you can handle this? Just stay comfortable instead . . ."*

At the same time, the voice of *courage* counters, **"I got this! Let's be bold and go for it!"**

These opposing forces—confidence versus doubt, growth versus complacency—clash in an internal dialogue, creating a tug-of-war that will ultimately shape your actions

When I contemplated resigning from an uninspiring job to pursue my passion for writing, I found myself trapped in the same inner turmoil many of us know all too well. On one side, **the voice of logic** argued for financial safety and stability. It made perfect sense: Why would I risk everything for the uncertainty of a writing career? But on the other side, **my artistic spirit** kept pushing me toward the leap. It whispered, "If you betray your gift, you betray yourself."

Through intentional self-dialogue, I found clarity. By releasing the assumption that external security automatically equals inner peace, **inspiration won out**. My mental conversations transformed, and with it, so did my actions. I took the leap because, after all, **if I didn't trust myself, who would?**

Shifting the Narrative

By directing focused awareness inward, we can consciously shift restrictive thoughts into empowering ones. This is not just positive thinking—it's deliberate, self-guided transformation.

Here's the key: **Every internal conversation matters**. Every act of self-questioning, every moment of self-encouragement or self-correction shapes the life we live. As we consciously edit the narrative in our minds, turning self-doubt into self-belief, **we rewrite our story.**

Here are a few things to keep in mind:

1. Catch yourself in the act. Pay attention when negative or limiting thoughts arise. Notice the tone of the mental conversations happening in the background.

2. Interrupt the pattern. When doubt starts pulling you backward, interrupt the flow. Say to yourself, "This doesn't serve me. What if I looked at this differently?"

3. Replace doubt with possibility. Just as you would rewrite a sentence to make it clearer, rewrite the thoughts that hold you back. Instead of "I'm not good enough," try, "I have the potential to grow and succeed."

4. Be the narrator of your own life. Take charge of the story you're telling. Make your inner dialogue a source of empowerment rather than sabotage.

Creating Your Mental Narrative

Imagine a movie where the protagonist constantly doubts their ability to succeed, where the narrator casts them in the light of failure and self-sabotage. Now, imagine the same story, but with the narrator speaking of resilience, courage, and potential. Which story do you want your life to mirror?

You are both the protagonist and the narrator of your life. The inner conversations you're having now, in this very moment, are the scriptwriters of your future.

Remember, life isn't just happening to you—**you're creating it.** Your internal dialogue shapes your external reality. By embracing this truth, you can steer the course of your life toward the visions that once seemed distant and unreachable.

It's time to become the director of your mental conversations. As you shift your self-talk toward growth, possibility, and empowerment, watch as your **external world begins to transform**

As you take ownership of your inner dialogue, **you take ownership of your destiny.**

The Consistent Mindset Always Wins

Have you ever wondered why some people seem to ride a continuous wave of success while others are caught in the highs and lows of an emotional rollercoaster? Let's explore the art of *consistency* together. Picture this scenario: two colleagues, **Joann and Alex**, are assigned the same challenging project.

Joann's productivity mirrors her emotional state. On good days, she's a powerhouse, tackling tasks with enthusiasm. But when obstacles arise or her mood dips, her focus falters. The project's progress moves forward in surges and stalls, creating a scattered and uneven path toward completion.

Now, consider Alex. Steadfast, methodical, and unaffected by emotional turbulence, Alex pushes forward at a consistent pace. Challenges don't derail his momentum. Instead, each hurdle is met with resilience, and he continues to move toward the goal with unwavering dedication.

The difference between Joann and Alex isn't talent or intelligence—it's their **mindset**. Joann is swayed by momentary emotions, while Alex embodies consistency. Through their stories, we uncover the secret ingredient to lasting success: the ability to show up and persist, no matter what emotions, setbacks, or external factors come into play.

Consistency: The Underestimated Superpower

Consistency, though often overlooked, is a **powerful force** that propels individuals toward their goals. Let's look deeper into Joann's approach. On the days when she feels inspired, she works diligently. But when doubt creeps in or motivation fades, her commitment wanes. The result? A start-stop rhythm that sabotages long-term progress.

Now, shift the focus to Alex. Unlike Joann, Alex's progress doesn't rely on how he feels in the moment. Whether he's excited or facing frustration, he keeps working. There are no highs and lows, just steady progress toward the goal. The project moves forward consistently, a testament to Alex's **unshakable discipline** and focus.

What sets them apart is simple but profound: **Alex prioritizes his objectives over his emotions**, while Joann lets her feelings dictate her actions. This key difference—**the ability to remain resolute and steadfast in the face of adversity**—is what separates those who achieve lasting success from those who falter.

The Trap of Emotional Inconsistency

For many, **emotions** are the driving force behind their actions. When they feel positive, they're unstoppable. But the moment negative emotions—doubt, fear, frustration—arise, their energy and focus evaporate. This **emotional volatility** is the trap that inconsistent individuals often fall into.

But those with a consistent mindset approach things differently. They recognize that emotions are **temporary**, and they don't let those fleeting feelings derail their progress. Instead, they maintain their focus on the goal, no matter what.

This is the key takeaway: **When you prioritize consistency over emotional reactions, you create a foundation for real, lasting success.**

Power of Consistency

So, how do you **cultivate** consistency in your own life? It begins with understanding its importance, but real transformation happens when you actively incorporate **key principles** into your daily routine. Here are a few strategies to help you build and maintain consistency across all areas of life:

1. Define Clear Goals

Set specific, measurable goals for both the short and long term. A clear vision provides a **roadmap** for where you're headed, helping you stay focused when challenges arise.

2. Prioritize Tasks

Identify the most important tasks that contribute directly to your objectives. By tackling these tasks first, you ensure that your energy and time are spent where they matter most.

3. Establish Routines

Create **daily or weekly routines** that align with your goals. Routines are the building blocks of habits, and habits foster consistency. Over time, your routines will carry you forward, even on the days when motivation is low.

4. Maintain Discipline

Discipline is the bridge between goals and accomplishments. Cultivate self-discipline to keep yourself on track, even when faced with distractions or obstacles.

5. Learn from Setbacks

View setbacks as opportunities to learn, not reasons to quit. Analyze what went wrong, make adjustments, and use those lessons to fuel future growth. Resilience is key to maintaining consistency.

6. Stay Positive and Motivated

Cultivate a **positive mindset** and surround yourself with motivating influences. Use positive affirmations and reminders of your progress to reinforce your commitment.

7. Track Your Progress

Keep a record of your progress and regularly review it. Seeing how far you've come can be incredibly motivating and serves as a reminder of the power of consistency.

The Power of Small, Consistent Actions

Consistency isn't just about grand gestures or massive efforts. It's about **small, consistent actions** taken day after day. Consider brushing your teeth: doing it once or twice won't make a difference, but doing it every day for years? That's when the results show. The same applies to anything worth achieving in life.

Imagine you're trying to grow a plant. Watering it once or twice won't yield results. But watering it regularly, even just a little bit at a time, nurtures its growth and eventually leads to it blooming.

It's **the regularity of small efforts that leads to great results.**

The Secret of Alex's Success

Now, let's return to our story of Joann and Alex. What truly makes Alex succeed isn't extraordinary talent or an easy path. It's his *consistency*. He shows up every day, ready to work, regardless of how he feels. His actions aren't dictated by emotion; they're guided by **purpose**. He understands that success is built one brick at a time, and each small effort contributes to the larger structure of achievement.

Joann, on the other hand, is talented and motivated, but her inconsistency holds her back. Her efforts are often intense but short-lived. She surges forward when the mood strikes but falls behind when challenges arise. This start-stop cycle leaves her feeling frustrated and stuck, even though she works hard.

Alex wins because **he never stops moving forward**. Whether he's taking small steps or large strides, he's always progressing. And over time, those small steps add up to significant milestones. **Consistency, not occasional brilliance, is the secret to lasting success.**

Become a Fan of Synchronicity

In the whirlwind of daily life, it's easy to overlook the subtle threads that tie everything together. We often write off certain events as random or insignificant, failing to see the intricate design connecting each moment. But what if, instead of randomness, there was meaning in everything? **Synchronicity** suggests exactly that—**the idea that life is filled with interconnected events, all carrying purpose and significance, even if we can't immediately see it.**

Imagine life as a massive puzzle where every piece, no matter how small or seemingly unimportant, fits perfectly into the larger picture. When we step back and take in the whole, those disjointed parts start to reveal a beautiful image we couldn't see up close.

Have you ever met someone at just the right time, as if the universe placed them in your path for a reason? Or have you experienced a series of events that seemed to fall into place so seamlessly it felt like magic? These are the moments when synchronicity shines through—**the extraordinary hidden within the ordinary.**

A Real-Life Example of Synchronicity

Take, for instance, a simple moment in your day—running into an old friend while getting coffee. It feels like a casual, random encounter at first, but then you find out that this friend works in a field you've been eager to explore. Over coffee, they introduce you to someone who opens a door to a new job, launching you onto a path you've been trying to find for years. Was it random?

Or was it synchronicity, guiding you to the right place at the right time?

Life is constantly creating these kinds of connections, even if we don't always recognize them immediately. And the beauty of synchronicity isn't in overanalyzing every small detail; rather, it's in **trusting that there's purpose and meaning in what we experience—even when we don't fully understand it.**

Shifting Your Perspective

The key to unlocking synchronicity in your life is simple: **shift your perspective**. Instead of viewing events as mere coincidences, see them as meaningful intersections. Begin to trust that everything—even the seemingly trivial encounters—plays a part in a larger, orchestrated story.

When you open yourself to synchronicity, life feels richer. You become attuned to the moments that once seemed random and start to appreciate how they fit into the broader narrative of your journey. The sense of purpose deepens, and you begin to feel as if you are always in the right place at the right time, surrounded by hidden opportunities.

Trust the Process

Embracing synchronicity doesn't mean trying to force meaning into every little thing. It's about **letting go of control and**

trusting that the universe has a plan—even when you can't see it. When you begin to view life through this lens, confidence replaces doubt, and you move forward with a sense of calm assurance, knowing you're a part of something bigger.

Take, for example, my friend Logan. He was stuck in a rut, trying to make a name for himself in the writing world but feeling like his big break was a million miles away. One day, while flying back from a work trip, he struck up a conversation with the person seated next to him—an editor. At the time, it felt like small talk, but little did Logan know this connection would later lead to a guest article opportunity that would change everything. That article? It went viral, catching the attention of a publisher who offered him a book deal.

Looking back, Logan could trace the entire series of seemingly "random" events that led him to that moment. From chatting with a stranger on a plane to writing an article that caught fire online, the path was anything but planned. Yet, each step was part of a **synchronized web of opportunities** waiting to be unveiled.

Embracing the Magic of Life's Connections

Watching Logan's journey unfold taught me an invaluable lesson: when we stop resisting the unknown and release our need for control, we open ourselves to the magical connections happening around us. Life becomes an adventure—a series of surprising twists where each piece of the puzzle, no matter how unexpected, fits into a greater masterpiece.

By becoming a fan of synchronicity, you'll find that **life is far more interconnected than it seems.** The more you trust the process, the more you'll witness incredible, "coincidental" events guiding you exactly where you need to go.

So, the next time something unexpected happens, whether it's a chance meeting or an opportunity falling into your lap, pause for a moment. Reflect on the bigger picture. Perhaps the puzzle pieces of your life are starting to fit together in ways you hadn't imagined. **Trust that unseen forces are at work**, and embrace the possibility that every moment carries a hidden purpose.

When we learn to see life through the lens of synchronicity, we stop seeing ourselves as passive observers of random events and begin to recognize that we are active participants in a grand design. The universe is always conspiring for your growth and success—are you ready to become a fan of its extraordinary connections?

Key Takeaways

1. **Transforming Adversity into Growth:** Adversity has the potential to be a catalyst for personal growth and positive transformation.

   Individuals who faced setbacks turned challenges into opportunities for resilience and self-discovery.

2. **Resilience in Action:** Resilience is not just about enduring trials; it involves using challenges as a means for personal and emotional growth.

   The stories illustrate how resilience can be a guiding force in navigating through life's difficulties.

3. **Conscious Overcoming:** Overcoming adversity requires a conscious effort to reframe setbacks as opportunities for rebuilding and reinvention.

   Embracing change and uncertainty can lead to unexpected gifts and renewed perspectives.

4. **Community and Support:** Connecting with support groups and communities can normalize challenges and provide strength during difficult times.

Sharing experiences with others can be a powerful tool for healing and growth.

5. **Continuous Evolution:** Viewing oneself as a continually evolving work-in-progress rather than a fixed end product allows for adaptability and self-trust.

Each challenge offers a chance for new perspectives and a deeper understanding of oneself.

Bonus Chapter:

Are You Ready to Expand Your Lens?

Author's Point of View

In this chapter, the author emphasizes a profound truth: **changing your perspective can transform your life experience**. They reference Wayne Dyer's powerful quote, "If you change the way you look at things, the things you look at change," highlighting how our perception shapes our reality. While the essence of things like love, trust, and other universal concepts remains constant, our **individual understanding** of them is what changes.

The author goes deeper, suggesting that **we are more than we realize**—our current experiences are a reflection of the energy we are putting out into the world. You attract what resonates with your current frequency or vibration. This means that **your inner state shapes your external reality**. If you elevate your frequency, you'll begin to attract and perceive things that align with that higher vibration.

To help guide the reader through this shift in perspective, the author introduces a chart inspired by Daryl Anka's teachings. These principles offer a roadmap to understanding life in a more expansive, holistic way. The author invites readers not only to see things differently but also to **embrace their unique perspectives**—to integrate all experiences as part of their individual journey.

Chart: Basic Principles of Life

1. **You are a non-physical consciousness having a physical experience.**

   - Your true essence goes beyond your physical body. You are a spiritual being temporarily living in the physical world.

2. **Your essential essence is unconditional love, and ecstasy is your birthright.**

   - Love and joy are not things to be earned; they are your natural state. Embracing this truth can lead to a deeper sense of fulfillment.

3. **The highest purpose of your life is to be yourself and live each moment fully.**

- Your life's mission is to authentically express who you truly are, embracing each moment as an opportunity for growth.

4. **You always have free will and the freedom to choose.**

    - Regardless of circumstances, you hold the power to choose your path. Your decisions shape your reality.

5. **Anything you can imagine that aligns with your life's theme is possible for you to experience.**

    - Your imagination is a tool for creating your reality. If you can envision it, and it aligns with your purpose, it is achievable.

6. **Your life's experiences are attracted through your strongest beliefs, emotions, and actions.**

    - What you focus on most becomes your reality. Your beliefs, feelings, and actions are magnets that draw in corresponding life experiences.

7. **Excitement is the physical translation of your true, core being. Follow your excitement.**

    - When you feel excitement, it's a signal from your higher self, pointing you toward your purpose. Following that excitement is key to aligning with your true self.

8. **You are naturally abundant, and your choices are always supported by creation.**

    - There is an infinite supply of abundance available to you. The universe supports your choices when you act in alignment with your higher purpose.

9. **There is only one moment in creation. Everything is the same thing from a different point of view.**

    - Time, as we understand it, is an illusion. Everything happens in the eternal present. Multiple perspectives coexist within this singular moment.

10. **You are an eternal being, and although you may change form, your consciousness cannot cease to exist.**

    - Your physical body is temporary, but your consciousness is eternal. You continue beyond this lifetime in various forms and experiences.

Source: *These basic principles of life above are inspired by the teachings of Bashar, as channeled by Darryl Anka, which emphasize concepts such as the nature of consciousness, free will, following excitement, and the creation of reality through belief and intention. For further insights, you may refer to Bashar's materials in "Blueprint for Change" and other works available through Bashar Communications.*

Embracing a New Perspective

The author explains that understanding these principles can lead to a profound shift in how you live. They encourage readers to start asking the question: "*What's your perspective on (insert subject)?*" Whether it's a relationship, a challenge, or an opportunity, this question invites exploration into how your current viewpoint might shape your experience.

By actively expanding your lens, you become aware that every experience, whether joyful or painful, holds meaning. Life stops feeling random and begins to feel like a purposeful flow of events guiding you toward your higher self.

A New Reality Awaits

The principles listed in the chart are not abstract ideas but tools to **apply in daily life**. The author encourages you to reflect on where your perspective might be limiting you. What beliefs are shaping your experience? Are you following your excitement, or are you letting fear and doubt guide your choices?

By shifting how you perceive the world, you open the door to **unimagined possibilities.** When you recognize that you are the creator of your reality, you stop being a passive observer and start living as an empowered co-creator. Your life becomes a reflection of your inner world, and as your consciousness expands, so does your experience of life.

Ultimately, the question isn't just about seeing things differently—**it's about living differently**. Each of the principles is an invitation to trust your path, embrace your potential, and realize that **you are far more powerful than you've been led to believe.**

So, are you ready to expand your lens and step into a life where **every moment is filled with purpose**? The choice is yours, and the universe is always supporting you, waiting for you to fully step into your power.

Author's POV: Interview Questions

Interviewer: What are your thoughts on the whole idea of Past, Present, and Future?

Author's Response: You see, the past, present, and future are things we've made up. It's like a human invention in our current world. Eckhart Tolle, in his book *The Power of Now,* brings up an interesting point—nothing really happens outside of the present. The past? It took place in the now. The future? Well, it's going to happen now.

Let me share a perspective that might change how you look at things. **Your life can get a whole lot better when you start seeing that your past doesn't determine where you are now (your present).** A lot of people think their past is why things are the way they are now. They get stuck in this loop, constantly trying to fix their past so they can feel stable in the present. But here's the twist: **Your present is the powerhouse.** You shape your past from the present—not the other way around.

When you focus too much on this so-called "past," all you're doing is recreating it in the now. **You're the creator of your past and the architect of your projected future—all from this very moment.** This makes us pretty powerful creators.

Your actions in the now are what actually predict where your life is heading.

Once you embrace this model, your past becomes something to examine—not to change it, but to see if you want to keep creating similar things now or just let them go.

No need to be ashamed of what happened during your exploratory phases. Your perspective at any moment aligns with where your mind was at the time. Things you once created for yourself might not have been enjoyable, but now you can decide to skip those same patterns. And sure, some lessons might take a few bumps on the head before you decide to switch things up, but the power is in realizing that *you* shape the narrative from the present, not your past.

Interviewer: Why do you call IMAGINATION the greatest tool ever?

Author's Response: Ah, imagination. It's like this hidden gem we all had as kids but somehow forget to use as adults. When we're young, we naturally use our imagination all the time, but life happens, and we start setting it aside. Well, here's the thing—**tap back into that kid-like imagination, and you're opening a doorway to endless possibilities.**

Let me share with you a method that's been a game-changer for me. I call it the **HIO method**, or the **Hand It Over method**. I learned it from a guy named Neville Goddard, who spoke about imagination as this incredible tool. He even said it's like having *Jesus Christ-level power*. The HIO method is about handing over situations to an imaginary version of yourself that you've created—the version of you living the life you want.

You might already be doing this without realizing it. **It's about using your imagination to create the life you want from the inside out.** A successful entrepreneur named Holton Buggs once said, "You don't get out of life what you want; you get out of life what you can picture." So, instead of just imagining that things around you will get better, picture yourself as the *best version of you*—living that life you dream about.

When you start acting from that imagined perspective, things around you start to change because your responses are different. This tool is all about making yourself better. I've seen it work wonders—people gaining confidence, getting promotions, launching businesses, fixing relationships, and so much more.

Imagination is like this secret doorway to endless possibilities. The best part? You don't have to go anywhere. It's all inside you. If you can imagine something, it exists for you in some way.

Neville Goddard used to share this story about a woman named Ann. She worked a tough job but used her imagination to manifest something as simple as a hat she really wanted. And guess what? **Ten days later, a friend surprised her with that exact hat.** That's the power of imagination—it literally shapes your world from the inside out.

So why do I call it the greatest tool ever? **Because it allows you to make the impossible possible.** It's like having your own superpower, a key you carry within. The trick is to remember you have it, and then use it.

Interviewer: What's your take on Trust?

Author's Response: Trust is basically having faith in a preferred outcome. I tend to avoid using the word "faith" because it's often thrown around in ways that can confuse its true meaning. Let me share a conversation I had with my friend Adam, and how a simple shift in perspective transformed his entire outlook on trust in his marriage.

Adam was in a rough spot. He told me, "I'm losing trust for her. I don't know how to trust her anymore. It feels like trust is just... gone."

Adam and his wife, Tonya, had been through some serious stuff. They had both cheated, and it left Adam feeling like trust had vanished. His wife seemed to have moved past it, but Adam couldn't shake the feeling that he couldn't trust her anymore.

That's when I told him something that changed everything: "**You never lose trust. Trust is always there. You're just placing it somewhere you don't want to.**"

I shared a concept from Bashar, who said, "*Doubt is not a lack of trust; it's 100% trust in what you don't prefer is going to happen.*"

What Adam was doing was trusting in the fear that his wife would hurt him again. Trust wasn't gone; it had just shifted toward the wrong outcome. He was at a 10 on the "trust scale"—but he was trusting in his worst fears, rather than what he wanted to experience.

I explained to him that trust is a constant, and where you choose to place it shapes your perspective. Adam realized that if he didn't adjust his focus, this pattern of mistrust would follow him into any future relationship. It wasn't really about his wife at that point; it was about the way he was interpreting trust.

This shift in perspective was what saved his marriage. He decided to stay and rebuild trust with his wife, not by forcing it, but by choosing to focus on trusting in the good—trusting in her efforts, in their commitment, and in their growth together. And this became his signature vibration from having practiced it for an extended point of time. They're still together today, learning and growing side by side.

Interviewer: Should we deal with pain? Is it needed?

Author's Response: Let's get right to the point: Pain is necessary. In fact, it's unavoidable. Everything in existence, including us, is exactly as it should be, and that includes pain.

Think about it—pain is a signal, a catalyst for growth. As human beings, we're naturally creative creatures. We crave newness, improvement, innovation. Once we've created the latest model of something, we're already itching for the next upgrade. It's not just about creativity, though. It's about the fact that we get easily bored. Pain reminds us of this constant push for more, for better.

We undergo surgeries to improve how we look, get tattoos to express ourselves, and dive into new technologies to keep life interesting. If we didn't experience pain, we'd likely create discomfort just to keep things interesting. I mean, think about it—without pain, who knows? We might twist our ankles for fun or invent even stranger ways to feel something in the pursuit of standing out.

But there's also meaningful pain, the kind we can't avoid. Think of a woman giving birth. Ask her if the pain was worth it, and she'll likely tell you yes without a second thought.

Here's how I break it down:

- **Physical pain:** can signal that something's wrong. It's a message from your body to get checked out, to heal.
- **Life's emotional pain:** can be a guide, pushing you to make adjustments, to grow, to evolve.
- **Relationship pain:** well, that can be the hardest, but it often signals areas in need of attention, helping us make decisions that are best for our well-being.

In many ways, pain isn't just helpful—it's necessary. Pain keeps us from getting too comfortable. It keeps us pushing toward something greater.

Interviewer: What's the deal with love? Tell us about that.

Author's Response: Love is universal—it's the same force, whether it's directed at yourself, your spouse, a friend, or family member. It's expressed differently, but it's the same essence. Many people think of love as a feeling that comes and goes, but what happens when that feeling fades?

Consider an elderly couple divorcing after decades, or a young couple calling it quits. Did the love simply disappear? Not really. Love doesn't leave; we sometimes bury it, suppress it, or cover it up. When we stop feeling love, it's often because we're choosing not to love ourselves fully at that moment. Love isn't something that others give us—it's a way we show up in the world, beginning within.

Maybe you've been hurt, built walls, or are holding onto regrets. But the love you feel comes from within; it's not a potion we need to find or give away. In her work, relationship expert Byron Katie explains that loving someone is more about who *you* are than about who *they* are. Our stories about others shape our feelings, but love is our responsibility. Expecting someone to love us is an unfair burden on them; it's our job to love ourselves.

Ultimately, when we love ourselves, we can truly love others. Love isn't something you choose—it's something you *are*.

Interviewer: Let's talk about relationships; what's your stance on that?

Author's Response: Relationships are something we all crave, whether they're friendships, romantic partnerships, or business connections. At their core, all relationships follow similar principles. They act as mirrors, reflecting back aspects of ourselves that we may not fully see or understand.

Think of it this way: if you're open to learning, relationships become powerful tools for self-discovery. Pay attention to what the people around you are saying or reacting to—it often reveals areas in your own life that might need growth or attention.

Take, for instance, a partner who brings up housework. If you really listen, you might realize they're not just nagging; they're actually reflecting something you already know deep down—that you could contribute more. This kind of awareness can lead to a better understanding of yourself and, ultimately, a stronger connection.

Now, here's a message for those who think happiness hinges on being in a relationship. You don't need someone else to complete your happiness. I recently congratulated my brother on his new relationship, and he told me he felt like he'd "found himself." My response? He became happy first, and then she showed up.

The takeaway here is to let relationships come naturally. What you're seeking is also seeking you, but it all starts within. Many people get it backwards: they look for a relationship while feeling broken or unhappy, which only attracts the same energy. So, it's no surprise when such relationships turn out to be turbulent or unfulfilling, repeating the same patterns and even passing them down to the next generation.

In essence, relationships are opportunities for growth and self-discovery. When you find happiness within yourself, you set the stage for truly fulfilling connections with others.

Interviewer: You knew this question was coming. Do you believe in God?

Author's Response: Absolutely! I believe that, on some level, most people do—even those who say they don't. Many people refer to a "higher power" or talk about God as an energy that flows through everything. Some see God as a heavenly father, while others even see divinity within themselves. Ultimately, we're all reaching for something extraordinary, something beyond ourselves. So yes, I believe everyone has some concept of God, even if we see it differently.

The real point of confusion and division often centers on Jesus—his existence, his role, and his relationship with God. People may debate prophets, scriptures, or historical events, but the real challenge seems to be in understanding what to make of Jesus. That's where beliefs really start to diverge.

Interviewer: Let's chat about the age-old question: Are men and women very different, especially when it comes to their energies?

Author's Response: On the surface, sure, there are obvious physical differences, and we often talk about men having one kind of energy and women having another. But here's the truth: deep down, it's all one energy. We label them differently for convenience, but what really matters is the balance of energies within each person. Essentially, there are two main forces: active and receptive, or positive and negative, if you like.

Let's break it down:

- **Male energy** tends to be more active and driven—it's the "get-up-and-go" force that propels you into action, taking on challenges headfirst.
- **Female energy** is more receptive and intuitive. It's about nurturing, listening, and being open to receive

Here's the interesting part: anyone, regardless of gender, can tap into both types of energy. Men aren't limited to just the active energy, and women aren't confined to the intuitive side. We all carry both within us, and we switch between them depending on the situation.

Let's dive deeper into these energies:

- **Positive Male Energy:** This is the team player who's enthusiastic, giving, and driven to make a difference. They're active and always looking for ways to contribute and change the world through action.
- **Negative Male Energy:** This is more about independence and self-interest. It's a solitary energy, focused on personal achievement. Not necessarily unhappy, but content with simply getting by and prioritizing self over others.
- **Positive Female Energy:** Imagine someone who's a traveler, a sharer of wisdom, someone who loves helping others and is open to new experiences. They're excited about life, eager to learn and connect.
- **Negative Female Energy:** This is a more withdrawn energy. It's about division rather than unity, preferring solitude and keeping insights to oneself. There's little interest in others' joy, and sometimes even a tendency toward creating drama.

Here's a secret: we all have both types of energy within us, and it's natural to switch between them. Ever felt like pulling back from the world for a bit? That's an example of tapping into your receptive, introspective side—what I'd call "negative female energy." It's a cue to take a step back, reflect, and recharge.

Interviewer: Now, let's talk about the Positive and Negative Forces.

Author's Response: Don't get caught up in thinking that positive is the "hero" and negative is the "villain." It's a bit more nuanced than that.

To start, let's clear up a common misconception: separation doesn't mean loss or rejection. It's more like taking a step back to gain perspective while still remaining whole. Let me share a perspective that's really resonated with me. Walk with me for a moment!

Imagine a world where there are no mirrors, and you're entirely alone. How would you grow or reflect on yourself in such a place, without other perspectives to consider?

Interviewer: It wouldn't be possible to do so.

Author's Response: Exactly! Before mirrors, before other people, the challenge of self-reflection existed. How could anyone grow or understand themselves without some form of reflection? That's where the concept of separation comes in. Imagine that God, or the Universe, wanted to truly understand itself. So, it divided itself into countless parts, creating different perspectives for the purpose of self-reflection. It wasn't a rejection or a breaking apart—it was a conscious choice to experience itself in a deeper, more multifaceted way.

As physical beings, we're part of this cosmic self-reflection. Separation isn't about distance or disconnection; it's a natural process that allows the oneness to view itself from countless unique angles.

Some people might mistake separation for divine distance or even disapproval. But really, it's about enriching the oneness with a variety of viewpoints. Each of us represents a unique facet through which the oneness can explore and understand itself more fully.

In this vast, interconnected universe, we are all like mirrors, each offering a unique reflection. This diversity of perspectives creates a richer, more complete understanding of existence. Separation, then, is not a barrier—it's a bridge to deeper self-knowledge.

Interviewer: Hmmm. Interesting!

Author's Response: So let's go back to when God—or the Universe, if you prefer—separated a part of itself for self-reflection. Out of this split, we got a range of forces, and one of the most significant pairs is what we're discussing here: the positive and negative forces.

The **positive force** is like a cosmic glue; it's integrative. People who resonate with this energy feel that everything and everyone is connected in a vast, interconnected web. Their actions are often guided by love, compassion, and a sense of unity—they see and honor that divine connection in themselves and others.

On the other hand, the **negative force** operates through disconnection; it's segregative. It's about resisting or even rejecting the idea of universal connectedness. Those who align with negative energy are exploring separation, individuality, and opposition to the collective.

But here's the important part: negative energy isn't the "bad guy." It's simply a force that pulls us away from our true essence, which is inherently connected to the whole. Think of it as a temporary forgetting of our divine connection—a kind of spiritual amnesia that allows us to explore individuality in contrast to unity.

Yes, negativity has led to destructive behaviors and painful chapters in history, like slavery and violence. And we all experience moments of negativity—it's part of the human journey. But the point isn't to label positive as "good" and negative as "bad." It's about understanding the full spectrum of our emotions and experiences, and learning how to reconnect with that sense of unity and love within ourselves.

Interviewer: I'm not just going to let you gloss over this self-reflection concept dealing with God. Tell me more!

Author's Response: Sure thing! Think about mirrors. They show us things about ourselves that we might not see otherwise—from the way we look to what's going on deep inside. Mirrors reveal details we'd miss on our own. The people in our lives function in a similar way; they reflect parts of us that we can't see by ourselves. They bring different perspectives, showing us sides of who we are that we might otherwise overlook.

Without these "mirrors" in other people, we'd miss out on valuable reflections that help us grow. Feedback, even when it's challenging, is essential for self-awareness. When perspectives clash, it creates a kind of tension that can push us to evolve—just like how positive and negative charges balance each other out, or how constructive criticism sharpens and polishes our ideas.

Let me give you an example. I have a friend—we'll call him JC—who used to be really judgmental about his roommate's quick temper. He saw himself as the "rational one" and dismissed his roommate's outbursts as immature. But over time, he realized that this judgmental attitude was actually isolating him, not just from his roommate but from others as well.

Then he had a moment of insight: he recognized that his roommate was actually reflecting something back to him—his own buried anger. JC had never wanted to admit that he held anger inside, so he projected it onto his roommate instead. This realization became a turning point. He began to see his roommate's reactions not as flaws, but as a mirror for his own suppressed emotions. This mirror encouraged him to face himself, helping him become more self-aware and find healthier ways to express his feelings.

By letting go of the need to be "perfect" or always in control, JC started to understand that there are many ways people experience and express emotions like anger. He learned to speak his truth more openly, with respect for both himself and others. His roommate's emotional style ended up expanding JC's ability to be authentic and compassionate. Instead of insisting that his way was the only "right" way, he began to see these reflections as essential teachers in his journey toward wholeness.

This is part of the plan that God (or the Universe) set in motion. We're here to learn and grow through these reflections. Imagine if we all embraced self-reflection as a spiritual practice, something we're meant to do as part of the human experience.

The world would be a much better place if we looked at each interaction as a mirror, helping us become truer versions of ourselves.

Interviewer: How would you answer the question, "Who are you?"

Author's Response: I actually had a similar conversation on a podcast with some friends. My buddy John shared that he sees himself through his name and accomplishments, linking them to his sense of identity. Another friend, James, who's deeply connected to his faith, described himself as a child of God, made in His image. Both perspectives resonated, each reflecting a meaningful view of identity.

When it was my turn, there was a pause, like they were expecting something profound. Instead of going the conventional route, I decided to share a different perspective—one that dives into our spiritual essence.

I said, "Who am I? That's a powerful question, because it invites us to look beyond surface labels and roles." While I could have answered like John or James, I wanted to explore something deeper, something that speaks to our shared, spiritual core.

"At our essence, we are multi-dimensional, eternal spirits," I explained.

This perspective opens up a new way of understanding ourselves and others. When we recognize that our true identity is as infinite, unified spirits, it shifts how we see the world. The differences we see—our personalities, backgrounds, and choices—are simply expressions of the same underlying consciousness, manifesting in unique ways.

Think of consciousness like an ocean, with each of us as individual waves that rise and fall. We appear separate, but we're all part of the same vast, interconnected whole. This understanding leads us beyond temporary roles and titles, taking us back to the source of our identity—the eternal spirit that animates everything.

Acknowledging our shared essence brings a profound shift in perspective. Suffering feels less overwhelming, as we realize it's just one layer of experience. Our purpose shifts from achieving external success to expressing higher virtues like love, compassion, and truth. And every encounter becomes an opportunity to honor the divine spirit in ourselves and others.

Interviewer: So, in general, what do you think about life?

Author's Response: Well, here's how I see it: in life, the rules aren't as fixed as we often think they are. It's a bit like that famous scene from *The Matrix*, where the kid says, "There is no spoon." That line gets at something profound—what we perceive as solid reality might not be as unchangeable as it seems. Life is a mind-bending experience, but we get so caught up in thinking everything is set in stone. Just like Neo learns to see beyond the illusions, sometimes we have to question what's truly "real." When you start to wonder, "Is the spoon really there?" it opens up a whole new way of looking at the world.

Exploring this idea of "no spoon" is about recognizing that many of our limitations are self-imposed. It's like waking up to the fact that the so-called rules of life aren't carved in stone—they're more like guidelines drawn in sand. Life becomes this expansive playground where you're not just a participant; you're also a creator. The code of life is constantly shifting, and your perception is the key to navigating it.

As you start to see yourself as part of this grand design, the boundaries and rules that once seemed rigid begin to blur. You realize you're not separate from life's unfolding—you're an essential part of it. And just like Neo bending the rules of the Matrix, you have the power to shape your own reality. It's about moving beyond the ordinary and stepping into a space where the extraordinary becomes possible. When you accept that "there is no spoon," suddenly, the possibilities are as limitless as your willingness to see beyond the illusion.

In this way, every setback becomes just another curve in the matrix—a chance to grow and evolve. The mundane transforms into the extraordinary when you view it with fresh eyes. The truth is, you're the magician in your own story, and the script is yours to rewrite. So why settle for the ordinary when the extraordinary is waiting just beyond the edge of your comfort zone?

Interviewer: What do you think about having expectations in life?

Author's Response: Funny you should ask—I was just talking to my former coworker, Trent, about his job. He's been there for four years now, even though he swears every day that he's going to quit.

He said, "The job's okay, but it feels like Murphy's Law in action—anything that can go wrong does, and it's just too much."

So, I asked him, "What are you expecting?" He sighed and said, "I just want a good day where everything goes as planned, just once."

Here's the thing: everything *does* go as planned… according to your expectations. Trent says he wants a good day, but if he's constantly expecting things to go wrong and preparing for the worst, guess what kind of experience he's setting himself up for? That's right—more of the same frustrations.

A lot of people hesitate to expect the best because they secretly doubt that good things can happen to them. But if you're going to expect anything, why not aim for the best? The truth is, you never really know what's around the corner. Expecting positive outcomes doesn't guarantee that everything will be perfect, but it does open you up to seeing opportunities and possibilities that you might otherwise overlook.

Expectations shape your mindset, and your mindset shapes your reality. So why not expect good things? You might just be surprised by what shows up.

Interviewer: You mentioned that consciousness is "played out." What does that really mean?

Author's Response: Let me break it down—it's not that consciousness is outdated or unimportant. It's more like every possible path you could take has already been laid out in advance, kind of like a map. Let me give you an example.

My buddy Geremy called me one day, completely distraught. After 12 years of marriage, his wife had just confessed that she'd been unhappy for a long time, had even been seeing someone else for two years, but now regretted it and didn't want a divorce. Geremy was torn up, unsure of what to do, so he came to me for advice.

I told him, "Look, whatever choice you make—whether you go through with a divorce or decide to work things out—that path is already set. It's 'played out' in the sense that each possible decision has its own course and outcome." I didn't tell him what to do because it's his journey, his decision. But knowing that each path is already there can be kind of freeing. It takes away some of the fear and anxiety because you realize that no matter what, there's a path for you—and you'll come out of it okay, one way or another.

Think of it like this: imagine God gives you a room. You're placed in this room, and no matter what you do, you're going to explore every corner of it eventually. But how you navigate within that room is up to you. You can sprint across it, redecorate it, invite friends over, or even dance through it—whatever feels right to you. The tasks and challenges set for you in that room will still happen, and they're designed to help you grow. The beauty is that, whatever path you choose, you'll come out of it with valuable experiences. Those experiences become your lessons, and now you're equipped to help others with what you've learned.

The key takeaway is that, just like with that room, life is a journey, and every choice you make is part of that journey. You have your own unique "room," and the adventures within it are all leading you toward growth and understanding.

Here's something to think about: every active decision you make, whether "good" or "bad," gets some level of support from the Universe. Even if someone chooses a negative path or ignores their higher purpose, the universe still supports that active choice. Have you ever wondered why some people, who don't seem to make the best choices, still end up successful or enjoying life? It's because the Universe backs up their active decisions. Now, just imagine the kind of support you'd get if you chose a path that truly aligned with your highest self.

This is what some people call the Law of Attraction—it's simply the Universe supporting your decisions, whatever they may be. So if you're intentional about your path, if you focus on the things that really matter to you, the support is there. Consciousness, in this sense, is a field of possibilities, and the path you choose to walk is always honored and supported.

Interviewer: Would you consider yourself successful?

Author's Response: Success is a journey, so here's how I'd put it: I'm successful whenever I achieve a goal. If I'm not actively working toward something, success doesn't really cross my mind. It's that sense of fulfillment when you get what you're aiming for. Some say success and happiness are linked, but I see them differently.

Success is something we pursue, a goal to reach, while happiness is something you already have inside. Napoleon Hill explained it well: "Success is getting what you want; happiness is wanting what you have." Often, we chase both as if they're running from us. Success is worth pursuing, but it doesn't need to be chased endlessly; timing matters. Happiness, though, is part of who we are—it's already within us.

Success is about hitting our targets and feeling the joy that comes with achievement. It's that excitement when you finally reach something important to you, whether it's a big work goal, buying something meaningful, or even the thrill of completing your to-do list. As a kid, saving up for a special toy felt like a huge accomplishment. As adults, achieving bigger goals gives us that same thrill, but these feelings are temporary. To keep feeling that satisfaction, we need new goals to strive toward.

On the other hand, happiness isn't dependent on achievements or possessions. For a long time, I thought happiness came from having certain things in place—good job, marriage, financial security. But I saw people with all of that who were still unhappy. I even found myself feeling unfulfilled despite having those things. I tried thinking positively, using affirmations, and changing my mindset, but the happiness was always temporary.

Then I read Michael Neill's "Supercoach," and it shifted my understanding of happiness. I realized I didn't need to change anything to be happy—happiness isn't something to attain; it's something that's always there. We often look to relationships, work, or other external things to make us happy, which can lead us to act against our values. But true happiness isn't found in external validation. When we focus on our own thoughts and beliefs, we see that we shape our reality, and that happiness is, and always has been, a natural part of who we are.

About the Author

Mister Rivers is a transformational life coach, self-discovery advocate, and the author of *Adjust Your Lens: How Shifting Your View Transforms Your Life and Empowers Others*. Committed to helping individuals break free from limiting beliefs, Mister Rivers inspires others to live with purpose and fulfillment.

In his early years, Rivers struggled with self-doubt and negative self-talk that affected his relationships and career. His search for answers led him to the works of influential thinkers like Neville Goddard, Daryl Anka (Bashar), Michael Neill, Mavis Karn, Sydney Banks, and Dan Koe. Through these teachings, he realized that his biggest obstacle was himself—and that by changing his beliefs, he could transform his life. This personal breakthrough inspired him to guide others toward the same realization.

As a certified life coach, Rivers brings a blend of wisdom, humor, and relatability to his work, helping others understand the mind-body connection and take charge of their thoughts. Through his book, *Adjust Your Lens*, and his transformative coaching programs, he empowers individuals to overcome past limitations and live with passion, purpose, and fulfillment.

Outside of coaching, Rivers has a passion for cooking, which he considers a space for self-discovery and connecting with others. His journey is a testament to the life-changing power of perspective and self-awareness, and he invites readers to embark on their own path to unlocking their potential.

Are You Ready to Transform Your Life and Empower Others?

As we conclude *Adjust Your Lens*, I hope these insights and techniques have sparked a shift in your perception of yourself and the world. Remember, the power to shape your reality lies within. By examining your beliefs, embracing new perspectives, and aligning your actions with your truth, you hold the key to a life of purpose and resilience.

Personal transformation is a journey, full of challenges and growth. Trust the process, lean into the discomfort of change, and know that each step—whether a stumble or a leap—is part of your unique story. You are the author of your life, the architect of your beliefs, and the master of your lens.

As you continue this journey of self-discovery, know you are not alone. A supportive community of fellow travelers, united in the goal of authentic living and positive impact, awaits you.

Together, we can encourage and inspire each other to live with intention and purpose.

I invite you to step boldly into the life you envision, empowered by the adjusted lens you've cultivated. Embrace your journey with curiosity, compassion, and commitment to personal growth. If *Adjust Your Lens* has resonated with you, I'd love to hear about your experiences. Reach out to me at *adjustyourlensbook@gmail.com* to share your story, ask questions, or connect with like-minded individuals.

If you found value in *Adjust Your Lens*, consider leaving a review, recommending it to friends, or sharing your favorite insights on social media. By spreading the message of perspective-shifting, you contribute to a ripple of positive change, empowering others to take charge of their lives and make a difference.

Thank you for being part of this journey. I'm honored to have shared these pages with you and look forward to connecting. Remember, your perspective is your power, and the world needs your unique lens now more than ever.

With gratitude and belief in your extraordinary potential,

Mister Rivers

www.ingramcontent.com/pod-product-compliance
Lightning Source LLC
Chambersburg PA
CBHW072148070526
44585CB00015B/1045